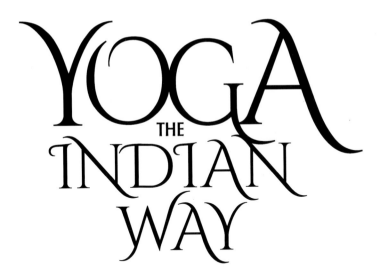

# YOGA THE INDIAN WAY

**Dharmavir Singh Mahida**

NIYOGI
BOOKS

Published by

## NIYOGI BOOKS

Block D, Building No. 77,
Okhla Industrial Area, Phase-I,
New Delhi-110 020, INDIA
Tel: 91-11-26816301
Email: niyogibooks@gmail.com
Website: www.niyogibooksindia.com

Text ©: Dharmavir Singh Mahida
Photographs ©: Dharmavir Singh Mahida
Editorial and Design: Write Media

ISBN: 978-93-85285-77-6
Year of Publication: 2017

Printed at: Niyogi Offset Pvt. Ltd., New Delhi, India

# CONTENTS

श्री आदिनाथाय नमोऽस्तु तस्मै योनोपदिष्टा हठयोगविद्या।
विभ्राजते प्रोन्नतराजयोगमारोढुमिच्छोरधिरोहिणीव॥ १॥

[I salute the primeval Lord Shiva, who taught Goddess Parvati the knowledge of Hatha Yoga, which is like a stairway for those who wish to attain the supreme Raja Yoga.]

# INTRODUCTION

Yoga, they say, is as old as time itself. It was practised in some form or the other by the gods and goddesses, sages and saints, gurus and teachers. Time moved on, and there were new beliefs and systems and, with them, came different poses and postures. From Lord Shiva meditating in Mount Kailash and Lord Krishna imparting the knowledge of yoga to Arjuna on the battlefield of Kurukshetra, yoga has extended its reach much beyond borders and boundaries. We now find new forms and methods, with yoga having become a global phenomenon. The marking of a special day in the calendar, June 21, as International Day of Yoga, further underlines its importance and value.

The word 'yoga' means to join, combine or fuse. That is, to combine body, mind, intellect to the soul (atma). The saints of India say that it is a process of connecting your 'unreal self' (body, mind, intellect) with your 'real self', the soul.

I strongly believe that yoga needs to be demystified. If the reader, who is a potential sadhaka (seeker), is well informed, he may take up and pursue the practice of yoga with conviction for the rest of his life. Otherwise, he may just give it up due to lack of priority, time, interest and so on. The background of philosophical knowledge given here is meant to ignite the fire within and keep it burning. It will encourage the reader to go to the depths of the 'self' and, at the same time, experience and appreciate the great, timeless contributions of this wonderful culture. To be able to achieve anything, you have to be equipped with the requisite knowledge and possess certain qualities before venturing ahead. This is the reason I have included essential topics such as Sankhya, Vedanta and Ayurveda, besides the yoga texts, in this book.

The scriptures say that it is rare to be born a human being and there is a purpose behind it, which is to realise oneself. The holy books reveal that this can be achieved by first fulfilling the four purusharthas (objects of human pursuit), also interpreted as duties—dharma (path of righteousness; artha (material wealth); kama (fulfilling desires); and moksha (liberation). The goal of achieving material wealth and fulfilling desires must be within the path of righteousness, which is mentioned in the scriptures. Following the path of yoga, step by step, helps to achieve this goal with proper understanding and a clear mind.

Man's evolution has been different at various times. With particular reference to the present, the changes he has undergone have been far too rapid, with the result that the balance which, for centuries, was in tune with nature has been lost. Sedentary lifestyles, the demands of the society we live in, especially with regard to materialism, unhealthy eating and drinking habits and, of course, the discipline that our system demands to function properly have undergone a swift change at the cost of our mental and physical health. In other words, we are constantly misusing the safety valves that are provided to this otherwise wonderful 'machine', leave aside the disrespect and thanklessness we display to our Creator.

The simplified, yet effective and safe, methods for practising yoga, as shown in these pages, are meant for almost anyone between the ages of 8 and 80 years. They are based on traditional practices. This book should not, however, be considered an instruction manual; you are expected to exercise your judgment and find out whether the practice brings positive changes in you and make modifications as per your personal requirements.

You may also well question whether there is need for one more book on yoga. It is true that there are several books already available on this subject and many have benefitted considerably from learning and practising yoga. People who are less fit, though keen on learning *asanas* (postures), give up easily after a few trials due to difficulty in achieving the right posture, lack of enthusiasm, lack of conviction, laziness and so on. Also, the aches and pains that afflict the less flexible body easily discourage them. They quickly forget that inspiration has to be followed by perspiration. This book is especially meant for them since it offers easy means and safe methods to practise *asanas* and Pranayama, however stiff the body may be initially. It also provides excellent guidelines to those who want to follow a spiritual path, but are confused as to where and how to start.

Teachers of yoga will find it useful to receive these guidelines to be able to offer more variety to their pupils. The younger generation, sportspersons and athletes have also been kept in mind as Surya Namaskar and a chapter on Dynamic Yoga has been included. These were introduced during my years of working with top athletes of the Armed Forces at their Sports Medicine Centre.

The strength of this method, which is explained along with illustrations in the book, lies in the judicious use of various items such as chairs, blankets or bed sheets, bolsters, cushions, beds, walls and so on, commonly found in every household. This assists the practitioner to bend or stretch his body with proper alignment and hold the poses for a longer period, thus achieving a higher level of anatomical, physiological and psycho-mental benefits.

This book is an effort to put the great science and art of yoga in its right perspective by describing its philosophical background in simplified terms without losing its essence. It also covers the practical part of yoga, which is so important for our spiritual growth. The intent is to motivate and guide the reader to become a seeker, who, in due course, gets a 'taste' of the fascinating experience of *ananda* (bliss).

The credit for the evolution of yoga goes to Padma Vibhushan Yogacharya BKS Iyengar, who, in the course of 80 years of dedication to this subject, developed innumerable methods to teach and inspire people like me to further create possibilities to help others. His emphasis on the importance of knowing the human system thoroughly, supported by his precise knowledge of practising *asanas* and Pranayama, has helped in the application of yoga for therapeutic purposes as well. Yoga is accepted as conventional medicine as the results speak for themselves. Thousands of people around the world are practising Iyengar Yoga and keeping themselves mentally and physically fit.

Earlier, when I was working in a private firm, my job demanded that I travel and stay in hotels. This did not, however, deter me from my daily practice of yoga, as I used all the furniture as props. Of course, I made sure that I did not break anything or dirty the walls! I often show my friends and students different ways to judiciously use the items at home, whenever I visit them. Improvised and easy-to-practice, alternative methods of getting into the required *asanas* and to be able to stay in them are suggested in this book, thus ensuring that the so-called aches and pains that irritate the beginner are relieved. These *asanas* not only bring immediate relief to the aching parts of the body but also rejuvenate and activate the entire physical and mental system, thus encouraging the practitioner to go ahead with the confidence and zeal to reap the benefits of yoga at all levels. Correct and uninterrupted breathing is a must. This good habit of continuous rhythmic breathing becomes a part of life, thus affecting the mind in all spheres of life. People are now realising that the mind and the body cannot be dealt with separately. Their interconnection and interdependence are proved beyond doubt. Thus, health consciousness is increasing these days and health clubs equipped with expensive equipment are proliferating. The purpose of this book is not to stop you from visiting health clubs or indulging in other physical activities, but to help you to understand your body and mind better, avoid injuries and develop an enhanced inner sensitivity. After all, among all the systems of physical exercises, *yogasanas* are unrivalled as they are safe, with long-lasting effects; they are preventive and curative; they strengthen the bones and muscles and are indeed 'multipurpose'. All the benefits that accrue from the practice of yoga are discussed in detail in the chapters on the different practices and postures. On the other hand, I do hope that this book will also help you to tread further on your spiritual journey.

There are many different types of yoga classes being held all over the world today, but a majority of them are conducted like a military drill with many participants, with varying degrees of stiffness, struggling to achieve a particular pose. Such classes are totally 'body-oriented'; this kind of practice does not fall under the category of real yoga. This book helps you to motivate yourself and practise in the confines of your own home with full awareness which, in turn, helps you to 'turn inwards', thus fulfilling the real purpose of yoga and also to reap its positive 'side effects'. Here, attention has been taken to include suitable types of *asanas* and Pranayamas for professionals who spend hours at the table. You may also refer to the chapter on therapeutic yoga. The Dynamic and Static types of *asanas* and Pranayamas can be included in the curriculums of schools, colleges, training institutes, sports academies and other institutions. A suitable circuit training programme can be derived from the practice sequences given here.

A sincere effort has been made to keep the *yogic* exercises and Pranayama simple and practical, based on tradition and my own practice and teaching experience of 30 years. The purpose, obviously, is not to turn people into *yogis*, but to help them understand, appreciate and 'taste' this ancient science that we have inherited from our ancestors. My aim is not to take you to climb Mount Everest, but to guide you to the Base Camp, at the very least.

Yoga has become increasingly popular. There is, therefore, need for proper theoretical and practical guidance, especially for those who are keen to derive the benefits of this wonderful art and science. It is high time that yoga is put in its right perspective as it has been grossly misrepresented and positioned mainly as a set of exercises for health and limited fitness catering to flexibility. This book elaborates the connectivity of yoga to Indian philosophy and the way of life, which, in turn, inspires and guides the reader to practise yoga not only to achieve physical health benefits, but to go beyond to explore the challenges of the body and the mind. To this end, easy-to-practise, but effective, *asanas* are explained and prescribed.

Almost anybody can learn and practise with the help of items which are available in every household, including walls, as they are used as props. This helps the practitioner to learn and stay in the postures longer to derive more benefits at all physical levels, thus resulting in greater confidence and ease in rhythmic breathing. Moreover, the instructions with illustrations given both for doing the poses correctly and the sequences mentioned in the suggested weekly plans, help to avoid injuries at all levels. The yoga students who have posed for the photographs are of different ages, gender and with varying degrees of flexibility, so that all members of the family are motivated to practise. The weekly plan also suggests a great variety each day so that there is no monotony. A section is dedicated to those who have physical problems such as pain in the knee, lower back pain, neck/shoulder.

For, ultimately, this book is for you—the seeker who makes yoga an intrinsic way of life.

# YOGA IN PHILOSOPHY

Philosophy is, without doubt, India's greatest gift to the world. We consider it to be a product of experience, based on the direct and personal experience of *yogis* (also known as *rishis* and *munis*). The philosophical speculation on the ultimate nature of truth and the practical method of realising this truth are both equally important. Philosophy was never conceived as merely a theoretical exercise for the sake of conceptual clarity. It was not meant for any particular class or gender. All the orthodox systems of Indian philosophy had a practical aim, which was to achieve the liberation of the soul through perfection. It firmly established the basic assumption that human consciousness or the 'self' is, in itself, pure and divine.

Indian philosophies have certain beliefs regarding human existence These are: the acceptance of the law of karma as the morally and causally determined principle of the individual's birth, lifespan and quality of life; belief in a cycle of birth and death; and the concept of liberation as the permanent state of freedom from this cycle.

There are six classical systems of Indian philosophy, known as *darshanas*, derived from the Sanskrit root word *drs* (to see). The *shad darshanas* are, therefore, six points of views. Although these schools vary, there is a kind of unity in them as they are different viewpoints of the 'one truth'. The six systems are:

- Nyaya: Founded by Gautama, it is the science of logic.

- Mimansa: Also called Purva Mimansa, because it deals with the *purva* (earlier) part of the *Vedas*. It was founded by Jaimini.

- Vaisheshika: Founded by Kanada, it is the evolution of knowledge leading to the realisation of the self.

- Sankhya: Founded by Kapila, it is pure philosophy and tries to harmonise the teachings of the *Vedas* through metaphysical reason. It is a systematic account of the process of cosmic evolution.

- Yoga: Expounded by Patanjali, among others. It has an integrated approach, teaching the aspirant to train his body and mind to achieve the goal of existence, which is liberation, trance or *samadhi*. It is totally a 'subjective' science.

- *Vedanta*: Or Uttara Mimansa, so called because it deals with the last part, or the end (or best) of the *Vedas*. The author of the *Vedanta Sutras* is Badarayana. *Vedanta*, which has won many admirers in the West, is the culmination of the Indian philosophical wisdom based on the teachings of the *Upanishads*.

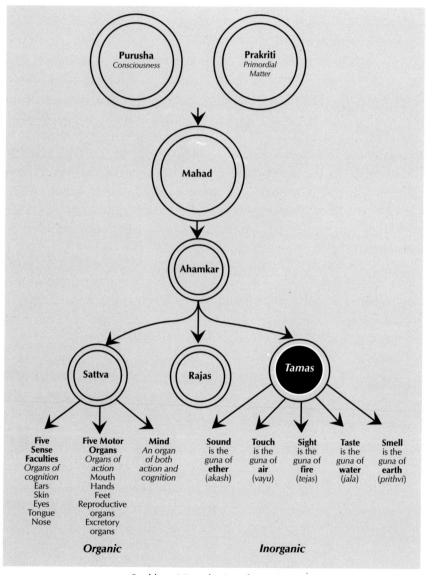

*Sankhya: Metaphysics of creation*

Yoga forms an integral part of all the philosophies of India. Sankhya and yoga are dependent on each other—Sankhya covers the theoretical part and yoga, the practical side. The former is also referred to as metaphysics by scholars. It attempts an explanation of nature as an immense complexity of elements that are ever-changing. This atheistic philosophy mentions the existence of two eternal realities, one being the *purusha* (consciousness) and the other *prakriti* (matter or energy as its manifestation). It begins with these and ends in the five basic elements (*panch mahabhutas*)—earth, water, fire, air and space.

The most effective and the easiest way of understanding Indian philosophy and its practical guidelines is by reading the *Bhagavad Gita*. A complete chapter (fourteenth) is dedicated to describing the *gunas* (attributes) and, in the seventeenth chapter, the three *gunas* are used for the comparison of the three types of *sraddhas* (faith). They play an important role as they form the 'bridge' between inorganic and organic matter and are also a part of us, as we are a part of creation (*prakriti*). The three *gunas* are: *sattva* (which is pure, buoyant or light and causes contentment and happiness); *rajas* (active, impels one to restless effort, but is needed to remove *tamas*); and *tamas* (inactive, creates resistance to activity and produces a state of apathy and indifference, leads to ignorance and sloth).

These *gunas* keep changing. A seeker has to understand why the *tamas* in the body has to be removed to bring in a balance with the mind, which is generally *rajasic* and needs pacifying to be able to ultimately get to the *sattvic* state. It is this balance that the practice of yoga brings about.

The etymological meaning of Sankhya is, 'that which explains very lucidly by analysis of the material of elements'. It is a systematic account of the process of cosmic evolution. One of its main principles is that the effect exists latently in the cause; therefore, development is to bring into light what is latent. For example, oil is contained in seeds, but it is necessary to press them in order to extract it. Strictly speaking, Sankhya does not conceive of an Omnipotent God, but it does not deny God either. The existence of God, it believes, can be established by logical proof (*purusha*), but there is really no necessity of bringing Him in. This can be well understood in the following example—if a yellow (or any colour) flower (representing *prakriti*) is placed next to a crystal (*purusha*), the crystal assumes a yellow taint, which, in reality, it is not. So is the condition of the human being. He sees himself as 'tainted', which he is not, being a part of *purusha*, that which is eternal. But, to realise this truth, yoga is needed to be understood, practiced and experienced.

The second chapter of the *Bhagavad Gita,* titled 'Sankhya Yoga', contains the essence of the scripture. This shows how important Sankhya is to Indian philosophy. Raja Yoga helps us to realise the principles of Sankhya. The aphorisms of Patanjali are the highest authority on Raja Yoga and form its textbook. He is said to be the incarnation of Sheshnag, the thousand-headed serpent on whom Lord Vishnu rests (as seen in Shayanasan). The learned sage has also written on ayurveda and Sanskrit grammar. A popular prayer (its beginning is given here) is attributed to him: '*Yogena chittasya padena vacham, malam shareerasya cha vaidya kena ...*' (The one who has given yoga for the realisation of the *chitta* [individual consciousness], grammar for the language [so that all that is mentioned in the scriptures can be properly interpreted] and ayurveda for purifying the body ... to such a saint we salute). Patanjali's system of yoga is known as Sheshwara Sankhya (the Sankhya philosophy that accepts God) as opposed to the Sankhya system that does not accept God (Nirsheshwara Sankhya). The *Yoga Sutras* are an excellent exposition on human psychology, guiding us to spiritualism.

Right in the beginning, in the second stanza (*sutra*) itself, Patanjali defines yoga as '*yogas chitta vritti nirodha*' (yoga is that which restrains the thought process [fluctuations] in the *chitta,* and makes the mind serene). His *Yoga Sutras* have gained tremendous significance among saints and scholars as they serve as a practical guide for spiritual awakening through remarkable psychoanalysis. The science of Raja Yoga intends to put before humanity a practical and significantly worked-out method of reaching the 'truth'. It proposes to give us a means of observing the internal states; the instrument being the mind itself.

Swami Vivekananda compares the mind to a lake. When the water of the lake is absolutely calm and steady, one can see the reflection of one's face in it, or a piece of stone lying at the bottom. When the water is disturbed by waves, this will not be possible. In the same way, when our mind is rising in the form of *vritti*s (waves of thought, or, literally, whirlpool), it is not possible to get a true picture of our 'real self'. The fluctuations in the consciousness are restrained. Simplified, it means penetrating to inner levels, from gross to subtle; signifying the complete course of action up to its ending in spiritual adsorption (*samadhi*). This state can be achieved by the practice of Astanga Yoga (Raja Yoga), the eightfold path.

There are eight limbs of yoga—*Yama, Niyama, Asana,* Pranayama, *Pratyahar, Dharana, Dhyan* and *Samadhi*.

- *Yama*: Restraint and keeping ethical disciplines. They are five *Yamas*— *Ahimsa*: abstention from all kinds of injury to life; *Satya*: truthfulness in thought, word and deed; *Asteya*: non-stealing, not even the desire to possess what someone else has; *Aparigraha*: not to hoard, non-receiving; and *Brahmacharya*: continence, behaviour in thought, word and deed, which leads to the Ultimate, Brahman (*brahmacharya* is also interpreted as celibacy).

- *Niyama* means observances and they are five in number—*Soucha*: purification, internal and external; *Santosha*: contentment; *Tapas*: austerity, fervour, burning desire, inner zeal; *Swadhyaya*: self-study and the study of the sciences of the self (scriptures); and *Ishwara Pranidhana*: surrender to God (although the source of this Raja Yoga is Sankhya philosophy).

Thus, *Yama* and *Niyama* form the foundation of yoga practice and are to be pursued every moment of your life. Even for those who claim not to follow a spiritual path, these ethical observances, along with yoga, build the person's character and free his mind of doubts, helping him to discriminate between what is right and wrong and thus develop *viveka khyati* (discriminating discernment). They will keep you mentally and physically alert and healthy and, along with single-pointed attention (*ekagrata)*, take you towards success in any endeavour.

- *Asanas,* at subtle levels, are meant to bring consciousness to different regions of the body so that their cells get activated and become more sensitive, thus playing a role in harmonising the whole human system (through the medium of chakras). At the gross level, they tone, fine-tune and strengthen the different systems that run our wonderful machine, the body, to help the mind create an internal symphony. Since the human system is extremely complex, it needs many kinds of postures to achieve this goal.

- The purpose of Pranayama is to cleanse the *nadis* (energy channels) and divert *prana* (a subtle system of flow of bio-energy in the body) to selected areas, such as the chakras, within the body. In Pranayama, one generally extends or prolongs or pauses in inhalation (*puraka*), exhalation (*rechaka*) and retention (*kumbhaka*). When the breath is stilled, the mind and consciousness are also stilled. We know that the mind and *prana* are closely related.

- *Pratyahara* means restraining or withdrawal of the senses; in this state, there is no interest left in external objects, resulting in total withdrawal to concentrate on the inner self. This is achieved only after practising the earlier stages of *Yama, Niyama, Asana* and Pranayama. According to Patanjali, the *bahiranga sadhana* (external quest) ends here.

- *Dharana* is a state of total concentration where all energies are channelised to a single point through *ekagrata*. The past, present and future become one. *Dharana, Dhyana* and *Samadhi* are known as *antaranga sadhana* [internal quest].

- In *Dhyana*, however, the *Dharana* stage is prolonged or continued. Its reflection thus becomes meditation. It just happens.

- *Samadhi* is in the *Dhyana* state of pure consciousness, paving the way for culmination into *samadhi*. According to Patanjali, out of infinite compassion for mankind, that is, by devotion and self-surrender to God (*Iswara pranidhana*), one can attain complete control over the mind, resulting in *samadhi*.

The *Srimad Bhagavatam* has various references to Hatha Yoga. The main texts on Hatha Yoga are *Hatha Yoga Pradipika* by Yogi Swatmarama, *Goraksha Samhita* by Yogi Gorakhnath and *Gheranda Samhita* by the great sage, Gheranda. They have been written and compiled between the sixth and the fifteenth centuries AD. In ancient times, Hatha Yoga was practised for many years for achieving higher states of consciousness. Now, however, the real purpose of this great science is being forgotten altogether. The Hatha Yoga practices that were designed and implemented by the *rishis* and sages for the evolution of mankind are being utilised in a very limited sense. Often, we hear people say, 'Oh, I don't practice meditation, I only practice physical yoga, Hatha Yoga.'

I would like to emphasise that Hatha Yoga is a very important science. Great yogis such as Matsyendranath, Gorakhnath and a few others in their tradition, found that some 800 years ago this science was being ignored by serious-minded people and was being taught falsely by others. Thus, they decided to separate Hatha Yoga, Raja Yoga and the practices of Tantra from the rest; they left out the rituals of Tantra altogether. That is how the system of Hatha Yoga was founded. It was during this time that Matsyendranath started the Natha cult, whose followers believed that before taking to the practices of meditation (Raja Yoga), one must be absolutely fit and should purify the body and its elements (especially the *nadis*). This is the theme of Hatha Yoga. In India, we believe that meditation is our highest goal, but we disagree on one point, that is, that one can immediately start meditation without any preparation.

The significance of the *Hatha Yoga Pradipika* lies in the fact that it solves a great problem of every aspirant. The author, Swatmarama, has completely eliminated the *Yamas* (moral codes) and *Niyamas* (self-restraints) that form the starting point in the Buddhists and Jain systems, as well as in Patanjali's Raja Yoga. Experience has taught us that in order to practise *Yama* and *Niyama*, one needs a certain quality of mind. We often observe that when we try to practise self-control and discipline, we are creating more mental problems in our mind. If there is no harmony in the individual, then self-control and self-discipline will create more conflict than peace of mind. This danger was clearly realised by the *yogis* and masters of Hatha Yoga. Thus, they proposed to discipline the body and went on to explain what they meant by the body. The subtle elements (*tattwas*) and the energy channels (*nadis*) within the body should be purified. The behaviour of the vital life force (*prana*), the entire nervous system and the various secretions in the body, should be properly maintained and harmonised. To this end, the *shat karmas* (six cleansing processes) were proposed.

The *shat karmas* alone, however, do not constitute the entire Hatha Yoga. Along with these, one should practice *asanas* and Pranayama. Self-control and self-discipline should begin with the whole body. *Asana* is discipline, Pranayama is discipline and *kumbhaka* (retention of breath) is self-control. One should try and sit in Padmasan (lotus posture) or any other comfortable pose, for 20 minutes; that is self-discipline.

The main objective of Hatha Yoga is to create an absolute balance of the interacting activities and processes of the physical body, mind and energy. When this balance is created, the impulses generated give a call of awakening to the central force (*Sushumna nadi*), which is responsible for the evolution of human consciousness. If Hatha Yoga is not used for this purpose, its true objective is lost.

The term '*hatha*' is a combination of two *beej* (seed) mantras—'ha' and 'tha'. It has been explained that, '*tha*' represents *prana* and '*ha*' represents the mind or mental energy. So, Hatha Yoga literally means the union of *pranic* and mental forces. When this takes place, a great event occurs in the human being. This is the awakening of the higher consciousness. The concept in Hatha Yoga is, therefore, to bring about a harmony between these two great forces (represented as *Ida* and *Pingala nadis*), which are on either side of the centrally located *Sushumna nadi*.

There is another difference between Patanjali's system of Raja Yoga and the traditional system of Hatha Yoga. The authors of the Hatha Yoga text were fully aware of the difficulty of controlling the fluctuations of the mind and they adopted another method. The Hatha Yoga texts state very clearly that, by controlling the *pranas*, the mind is automatically controlled. The vital force and the mind exert and influence each other. When the *pranas* are restless, it affects the mind and vice versa. By practising Pranayama correctly, the mind is automatically controlled. The authors of Hatha Yoga proposed another theme. They simple declared, don't worry about the mind, ignore it. Practise Pranayama, follow the *prana* through its vehicle, the breath.

The fundamental premise remains the same in all yoga systems— concentration and going within, using the mind and/or *prana*. To some extent, *shat karma* is the preparation for Pranayama and vice versa. Most people think of Pranayama as breathing exercises, but it is far more. '*Ayama*' literally means 'dimension', not 'control'. So, Pranayama is practised in order to expand the dimensions of the *prana* within you. If you want to achieve this transcendental experience, the practice of Hatha Yoga and Pranayama should be perfected and recommendations should be observed. This does not mean giving up all pleasures of life, but, at the same time, be aware that 'you can never have your cake and eat it too'. Once you have decided to step into another dimension of consciousness, you must be prepared to sacrifice some things (such as certain lifestyles) that are definitely detrimental to the practice of Pranayama and Hatha Yoga. Remember, the real reason you are practising

Hatha Yoga (*asana*, Pranayama, *mudra* [symbolic hand gesture] and *shat karmas*) is to develop the quality of human consciousness, not just the mind or the body.

You can never reach a point of evolution through intellect. As a matter of fact, intellect, at times, becomes a barrier to spiritual awakening and we have to find powerful means of transcending it. Hatha Yoga is most effective because you are working on the *prana* and bypassing the mind. The views expressed here are taken from *Hatha Yoga Pradipika*, published by the Bihar School of Yoga, Munger, under the guidance of Swami Satyananda Saraswati who was a direct disciple of Swami Sivananda Saraswati, whom I deeply venerate.

Hatha Yoga lays a lot of emphasis on what are popularly known as the *shat karmas—Dhauti, Basti, Neti, Trataka, Nauli* and *Kapalbhati*.

- *Dhauti* is divided into four parts—*antar* (internal) *dhauti*; *danta* (teeth) *dhauti*; *hrid* (cardiac) *dhauti*; and *moola shodhana* (rectal cleaning). These are further divided into two parts—*jala* (water) *basti* and *sthala* (dry) *basti*.

- *Neti* is a nasal cleansing technique and is divided into two parts—*jala neti* and *sutra* (thread) *neti*.

- *Trataka* involves a steady and continual gazing at a single point of concentration.

- In *Nauli*, you churn and isolate the abdominal muscles and organs.

- *Kapalbhati* has three practices: *Vatakrama Kapalbhati* (similar to *Bhastrika* Pranayama), which has now been made popular in every household by Swami Ramdev and is highly recommended; *Vyutkrama Kapalbhati*—sucking in water through the nose and expelling it through the mouth; and *Sheetakrama Kapalbhati*—sucking in water through the mouth and expelling it through the nose.

These cleansing practices are popular in India, but if they are not done under proper guidance, they may cause problems. That is why no instructions to practise them are given in this book. I believe that if we follow the basic principles of ayurveda (adhering to proper instructions for your daily routine and habits, especially of proper eating, according to the seasons) and *pancha karmas* (the five rituals of internal cleansing of the systems), where required, the *shat karmas* may not be essential.

An advantage of ayurveda is that a cleansing process from the *pancha karmas* can be selected as per the disturbed *dosha* (one of the three bio elements that make up our constitution) in the individual. All five of the cleansing processes may not then be necessary.

Patanjali's Raja Yoga and the Hatha Yoga scriptures have a common goal, which culminates in *samadhi*, the superconscious state. Hatha Yoga humbly claims to be preparatory to Raja Yoga. In reality, *samadhi* does not happen as a mere coincidence or by chance. As Swami Sivananda puts it, 'One gets a message prior to this state, which can be called divine intoxication.'

The culmination of this fascinating science of yoga can be best described in the following way:

Pure consciousness is Shiva, and His power is Shakti, who, in Her formless self, is one with Him. She is the mother of the universe, who as the life force also resides in the human body in its lowest centre, at the base of the spine, *muladhara* (known as the *kundalini*, coiled up serpent power). Shiva is realised in the highest brain centre, the cerebrum or *sahasrara padma*. Hence, yoga is the union of Her and Him (known as *laya*, assimilation) in the body of the aspirant where She rushes to be one with Him when 'awakened'. This results in the *jivatma* (individual soul), becoming one with the *Paramatma* (Universal Soul). This is the ultimate stage known as *samadhi*. The *Vedas* and the *Upanishads* also refer to this superconscious state as *ananda* (bliss).

The *yogic* scriptures mention chakras and *nadis*. The former are the *pranic*/psychic centres in the subtle body that are responsible for specific physiological and psychic functions. They are the conjugation points of *nadis*, which are astral channels (*sukshma*, subtle passages) made up of astral matter. It is through these that the vital force (*prana*) moves. As they are made of subtle matter, they cannot be seen. They are not ordinary nerves, arteries or veins. The source of all *nadis* is known as the *Kanda*, which is in the junction where the main *Sushumna nadi* is connected with the *Muladhara* chakra. It is from here that the *Sukshma prana* (vital energy) is carried to the different parts of the body. Some compare these to the meridians of acupuncture. In the gross body, the spinal cord terminates as a bunch of nerves as this astral centre is nothing but the *Kanda*. The *yogis* called the spinal cord the *Sushumna nadi*. It

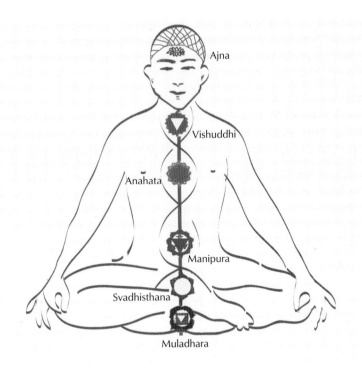

*The location of the six chakras*

is the most important of all the *nadis* as it connects the lowest chakra, *Muladhara*, to the highest, the *Sahasrara Padma*. The other two important ones, running to the left and right of it, are known as *Ida* (also known as *Chandra nadi*, which is cooling) and *Pingala* (also known as *Surya nadi*, which is heating). At the physical level, these two correspond to the two autonomous nervous systems. The flow of *prana* in them is completely involuntary and unconscious until controlled by *yogic* practices. The scriptures have different opinions about the total numbers of *nadis*, but it is certain that they are thousands of them.

The chakras, six in number—*Muladhara, Svadhisthana, Manipura, Anahata, Vishuddhi* and *Ajna*—are the junction centres of the *nadis*. These have corresponding centres in the spinal cord and the nerve-plexuses in the gross body. Wherever an interlacing of nerves, arteries and veins takes place, these centres are known as plexuses, which are well-defined in medical science. The vital energy that flows through them is considered as *sthula* (gross), whereas the *prana* that flows through the chakras is said to be *sukshma* (subtle). These two courses are closely interconnected as they influence each other. For, without the subtle body, the gross body is not possible. Therefore, each chakra has control over a particular centre in the gross body. All functions of the body, such as nervous, digestive, circulatory, respiratory, endocrine and so on, which have their corresponding centres in the physical body, are under the control of the chakras, which are all in the *Sushumna*. For example, *Anahata* chakra, which is in the *Sushumna nadi*, has its corresponding centre in the physical body at the heart (cardiac plexus). The personality of a human being can be directly correlated to the influences of his chakras on him. This has been also proved by aura photography.

*Kundalini* is what I would call the grand finale of yogic practice. The word *kundala* means coiled; its form is like a coiled serpent. The goal is to be achieved by awakening this *Kundalini shakti* that is lying dormant in the *Muladhara* chakra. But, it is easier said than done. To qualify, one has to do *Deha Suddhi* (purification of the body), *Nadi Suddhi* (purification of the *nadis*), *Manas Suddhi* (purification of the mind) and *Buddhi Suddhi* (purification of the intellect). The scriptures, the guru and yoga guide us in this process.

*Vedanta* (*anta* means end) means the culmination (or best) of all knowledge of the *Vedas*. To quote Swami Vivekananda, 'The knowledge of *Vedanta* has been hidden too long in caves and forests. It has been given to me to rescue it from its seclusion and to carry it in the midst of family and social life ... the drum of the *Advaita* shall be sounded at all places ... in the bazaars, from the hilltops and in the plains.' The *Vedanta Sutras*, also known as *Brahma Sutras*, were composed by Badarayana for whom they were eternal. The scriptures (*shastras*), lead to Brahman (the ultimate Truth, the Supreme Reality).

*Advaita Vedanta* holds the view that though there is one God, or *Ishwara*, there are many forms. There is a popular saying in India, 'What is but one, wise people call it by different names.'

In the words of Swami Vivekananda's guru, Sri Ramakrishna, 'As one can ascend to the roof of the house by means of a ladder, or a bamboo, or a staircase, or, in various other ways, so diverse are the means and ways to approach God.'

Today, synonymous to the word *Vedanta* is the name of Sri Adi Shankaracharya, who has walked the length and breadth of India to re-establish the authority of the *Vedas*. This holy text, the backbone of India, had been diluted owing to many reasons. This was around 1,200 years ago. Shankaracharya's compositions in Sanskrit are popularly recited and sung all over India. A masterpiece among them (also my favourite), is known as '*Nirvana Shatakam*' (six stanzas of salvation), which is the gist of *Vedanta* and can be summed up thus: 'I am neither the mind, intelligence, ego nor *chitta* (seat of memory); neither the ears nor the tongue nor the senses of smell and sight; neither ether (space) nor air, nor fire, nor water nor earth. I am eternal bliss and awareness, I am Shiva! I am Shiva!' This is the first of the six stanzas. Shankaracharya first clarifies by negation (what one is not) and, in the sixth stanza, ends up saying what one is: 'I have no form or fancy, all pervading am I; everywhere I exist, and yet am beyond the senses; neither salvation am I, nor anything to be known. I am eternal, bliss and awareness, I am Shiva! I am Shiva!' There were several saints after Shankaracharya who brought the great Bhakti movement to the fore. The spiritual thought was so deeply embedded in the people that even a few hundred years of slavery under foreign rulers could not destroy the spiritual culture which was prevalent since centuries.

The *Srimad Bhagavad Gita* also throws light on the other three yogas (besides Raja Yoga, which is known as the yoga of meditative path). They are: Karma Yoga (yoga of action), Jnana Yoga (yoga of knowledge) and Bhakti Yoga (yoga of devotion and total surrender). These yogas cannot be dealt with separately, as they complement each other towards the path of spiritual development in daily life. The *Bhagavad Gita* also encompases the three philosophical systems—Sankhya, Yoga and *Vedanta*. It was written as a practical guide by the great sage Vyasa some five thousand years ago and has been a source of knowledge that helps one to understand the complexities of life. The holy book clearly directs the reader to follow the path of spiritualism (liberation) and is meant for all, including saints, monks, scholars, seekers, common people (householders) and so on.

I want to pay a special tribute here to the 'father' of present day yoga and *Vedanta*, Swami Sivananda Saraswati of Rishikesh. His disciples are heading and serving various schools all over the world today, having drawn inspiration, guidance and encouragement from him. He systematised *asana* and Pranayama practice, making good use of his knowledge as a doctor. At the same time, he spread the teachings of the *Vedanta*. He also did not miss out on the *bhakti* aspect by introducing *kirtan* (devotional) singing in all his centres. Another personality in present times who has tremendously contributed to yoga and ayurveda is Swami Ramdev. He has spread this knowledge, both practical and theoretical, to millions in India. He, too, like Swami Sivananda, is the son of the Himalayas as his organisation is in Haridwar, a few miles from Rishikesh. Gurudev Jaggi Vasudev of Isha Yoga needs a special mention as he has created a storm in the field of yoga, especially in the English-speaking community.

My salutations to these masters and also to hundreds of those who are tirelessly working in the field of yoga and spiritualism. To them goes the credit of keeping the tenets of India's philosophy alive in our hearts.

# YOGA AND AYURVEDA

A yurveda is a holistic system of medicine indigenous to and widely practised in India. *Ayu* means life or daily living and *veda* is knowledge. Ayurveda, 'knowledge of life', is a science that helps an individual to gain sound health and an equally sound mind. It also prepares him towards achieving a desired spiritual goal. Another important aspect of ayurveda is that its medicines and herbs are unparalleled in the field of rejuvenation.

Like yoga, ayurveda is also derived from Sankhya, which teaches that man is a microcosm, a universe within himself. He is a child of the cosmic forces of the external environment, the macrocosm. Originating in the cosmic consciousness, this wisdom is believed to have been intuitively received in the hearts of the *rishis*. They perceived that consciousness was energy manifested into the five basic elements—ether (space), air, fire, water and earth.

This concept of the five elements lies at the heart of ayurvedic science (based on Sankhya). Thus, out of the womb of the five elements, all matter is born. These five basic elements manifest in the human body as three basic principles, or humours, known as *tridoshas*. These three—*vata, pitta, kapha*—govern all the biological, psychological and physio-pathological functions of the body, mind and consciousness. Thus, the *tridoshas* are the foundation of the psychosomatic existence of man.

The concept of *vata, pitta, kapha* is unique to ayurveda. *Vata* is the principle of movement; that which moves is called *vata*. All movements within the channels (*nadis*) to transport fluid, blood and nutrition is done by *vata*. This bodily air, or *vata*, may be characterised as the subtle energy that governs biological movements. It consists of two elements—space and air. A swami who has dedicated his life to serving people by helping them with ayurveda (he even grows the necessary herbs) once told me about a very interesting aspect of *vata*. We are aware that we have miles and miles of blood vessels and capillaries in our body. Disturbed *vata*, he said, forms bubbles in these and hence does not allow blood and energy to flow freely.

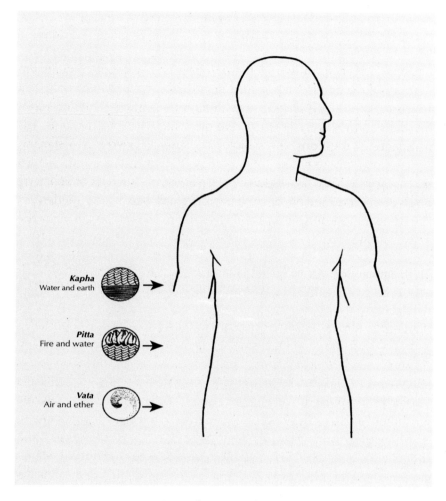

*Seats of vata, pitta, kapha*

The main seats of *vata* are the large intestine, pelvic cavity, bones, skin, ears and thighs. If excess *vata* accumulates, it has the tendency to dry up that area. *Vata* aids movements, including of fluids, allowing them to flow within the body. This is reduced as one's age advances and *vata* gets imbalanced.

*Pitta* means 'fire', which is a reference to the heat energy of the body. Its function is to provide warmth and transform nutrition to the required *dhatu* (anatomical component). The main seats of *pitta* are the small intestines, sweat glands, stomach, blood, fat, eyes and skin. *Pitta* governs digestion, absorption, assimilation, nutrition, body temperature and also intelligence and understanding. Psychologically, *pitta* arouses anger, hate and jealousy. It is formed from the two elements—fire and water.

*Kapha* is formed from two elements—earth and water. It cements the elements of the body which, in turn, provide the material for the physical structure. *Kapha* gives necessary nutrition for stability, it lubricates the joints, provides moisture to the skin, helps to heal wounds, fills the spaces in the body, gives biological strength, vigour and stability, supports memory retention, gives energy to the heart and lungs and so on. It is psychologically responsible for emotions such as attachment, greed and long-standing envy; it is also expressed in the tendencies towards calmness, forgiveness and love. The main seats of *kapha* are the respiratory system, chest, lungs, nasal passage, among others.

The balancing of the *tridoshas* is absolutely necessary for health, and vice versa, since imbalance inevitably causes sickness.

In the study of yoga systems through the ages, considerable importance is given to the *shuddhi* (cleansing) of *nadis* so that energy flow to and fro from the *Ida, Pingala, Sushumna* to the chakras (conjugation points of the *nadis*) is not hindered. Some yoga scriptures such as the *Hatha Yoga Pradipika* prescribe *shat karmas*, the six cleansing processes, which are rather tedious, as a precondition. Also common to all systems is the *shuddhi* that happens while doing Pranayama. The practice and understanding of ayurveda helps in bypassing some of these stages since most of the blockages, which are caused due to an imbalance in the *doshas*, improper diet and disturbance in the *agni* (digestive fire), are avoided.

The *pancha karmas* (five cleansing processes) are:

- *Nasya* (cleansing the respiratory tract)
- *Basti* (enema)
- *Vamana* (therapeutic vomiting)
- *Rakta moksha* (localised blood letting)
- *Virechana* (purgation)

These are easier as well as safer when done under supervision. The *vaidya* (ayurved practitioner) can decide, after ascertaining the disturbed *dosha/doshas*, as to which of these is required. It needs at least four to five days of preparation before they are done under supervision. The results speak for themselves. I tried them a few years ago and felt totally

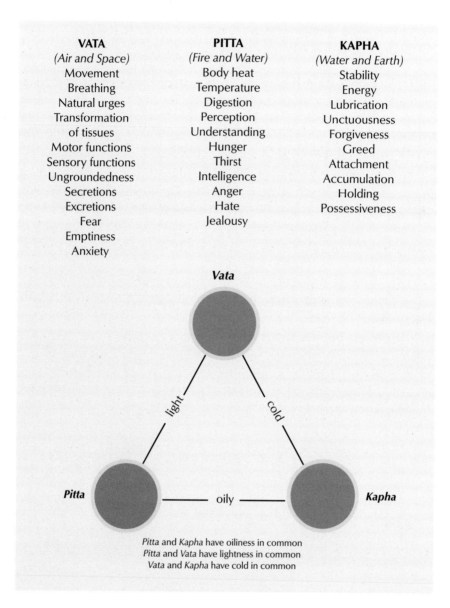

| VATA | PITTA | KAPHA |
|---|---|---|
| *(Air and Space)* | *(Fire and Water)* | *(Water and Earth)* |
| Movement | Body heat | Stability |
| Breathing | Temperature | Energy |
| Natural urges | Digestion | Lubrication |
| Transformation | Perception | Unctuousness |
| of tissues | Understanding | Forgiveness |
| Motor functions | Hunger | Greed |
| Sensory functions | Thirst | Attachment |
| Ungroundedness | Intelligence | Accumulation |
| Secretions | Anger | Holding |
| Excretions | Hate | Possessiveness |
| Fear | Jealousy | |
| Emptiness | | |
| Anxiety | | |

*Vata*

*light* — *cold*

*Pitta* — oily — *Kapha*

Pitta and Kapha have oiliness in common
Pitta and Vata have lightness in common
Vata and Kapha have cold in common

*Functions of the* tridoshas

rejuvenated. Ayurveda is a time-tested science by itself. We, with our present lifestyle, need to purify the body and the mind to begin with. We have toxins in our body from the accumulated *ama*, the undigested food that is already sitting in our system, especially in the intestine. These toxins are a source of diseases that may already be there or are waiting to manifest. Cleansing the *nadis*, which are carriers of subtle *prana*, is a far-fetched exercise and that is why I feel it is absolutely necessary to utilise the theory and practice of ayurveda to begin with.

The following *shloka* on complete health, which has been taken from an ayurveda scripture, is interesting:

*Samadoshaha samagnischa samadhatumalakriyaha Prasanna atmendriya manah swastha ityabhidhiyate*
[Whose *doshas (vata, pitta, kapha)* are balanced, *agni* (digestive fire) is balanced, *dhatus* (plasma, blood, muscle, fat, bone, bone marrow and reproductive tissues) are balanced, and waste products (sweat, urine and stool) are timely eliminated, whose *atma* (soul), *indriyas* (five organs of action and five organs of perception) and mind are joyful, is known to be healthy.]

This is similar to the World Health Organisation's definition of health: 'Health is a state of complete physical, mental and social well-being and not merely an absence of disease of infirmity.'

Yoga helps in this process, resulting in a state of joyfulness, where you are taken to higher levels of consciousness. Ayurveda, in turn, also helps in fulfilling the purpose of yoga in helping to balance the three *gunas* within us.

*Agni* needs special mention both in yoga and ayurveda as practising *asana* and Pranayama keeps it well balanced. One should follow *dinacharya* (rituals in daily life) and *ritucharya* (according to the climate), as mentioned in ayurveda. For example, food intake is a 'ritual'. This process is compared to *yagna* (fire worship) as it is an offering (*ahuti*) to the *agni* within. But, prior to this ritual, there are pre-conditions involved— one should have cleared the body (intestine, bladder) of all impurities; taken a bath; be calm and composed (obviously no talking!) and be seated in Sukhasan (cross-legged) and so on. Should we not reintroduce this ritual in our daily life?

In earlier times, a particular lifestyle and routine, as prescribed in ayurveda, was imbibed as a habit all over India. Obviously, each region had to adjust itself according to its historical, social, environmental and geographical compulsions. But, the local saints and *rishis* saw to it that the main goal of elevating the human being towards spiritualism was kept as a priority.

In concluding, I would like to stress that good habits are a way of life. Among these are:

- Getting up early (preferably an hour before sunrise).

- Drinking warm water.

- Evacuating bowel and bladder.

- Brushing teeth and rinsing the mouth.

- Bathing every morning; having an oil massage before your bath is highly recommended.

- Eating the right kind of food, depending on the *dosha* type and lifestyle. Vegetarian food, which is easy to digest, is best for spiritual development. The ayurveda rule is that one should 'feed' the fire only when it asks for it.

- Chewing food slowly, in silence, gratitude and with awareness.

- Eating light food at least two to three hours before going to sleep.

These are just a few tips; the rest depends on the commitment of the seeker. Yet these are essential for the well-being—spiritual and physical—of an individual. Ayurveda and yoga go hand-in-hand in keeping us healthy. Both acknowledge that keeping the body healthy is essential for life and living.

# ASANAS: PLAYING A VITAL ROLE

Yoga *asanas* were designed by saints and sages after many years of experimentation, observation and practise in varying conditions of environments, climates and locations and then passed on to the next generation. Practising is also a kind of 'weight training', using one's own body weight! The sages could thus withstand all sorts of onslaughts owing to climatic conditions. They led a tough life, with little nutrition. However, nothing could deter them from their journey to go 'within' and explore daring frontiers.

The positive effects, which are indeed numerous, come only when the *asanas* are performed in the correct manner and when one remains in the prescribed pose for a sufficient time. We have different anatomical systems functioning in our body—muscular, skeletal, circulatory, respiratory, endocrine, nervous, digestive and so on. It is the function of the *asanas* to help distribute energy equally to all regions of the body, thus activating various organs so that they are toned to function properly. At the same time, they recharge the whole system and do not dissipate energy like many other forms of exercises.

It is rare that all our muscles fully relax when not in use. Due to mental, physiological, habitual or anatomical reasons, muscles or a group of muscles have residual tension in them. While practising *asanas*, these are released or even balanced and, to a certain extent, strengthened after the release of the posture. When internal (residual) tensions exist, the impulses are carried through sensory and motor channels to the brain, back and forth, thus preventing a unidirectional flow of energy. This is essential to enter into a meditative state or perform any form of activity that demands full mental concentration. *Asanas* play a vital role in strengthening the peripheral muscles around the various joints as they also prolong the life of the joints by bearing and distributing loads during different static and dynamic movements that occur during the course of our daily movements or exercises. This creates a situation that is conducive for adequate lubrication in the joints. *Asanas* contribute greatly to the fine-tuning of the smaller muscle groups.

It is believed that during the course of man's evolution, the human spine has not yet totally adapted itself to the multifarious activities that we perform. Over and above that, whatever adjustments that nature has provided have been disturbed totally by the sedentary lifestyle of our present day culture. The biggest so-called culprits here are items of comfort such as sofas, tables and chairs as well as a lifestyle that provides 'luxury' to the present generation. These comforts have restricted the natural movements that human beings have been used to for thousands of years. The practice of *yogasana* helps to regain the lost movements in the joints and thus put a check to diseases such as arthritis. The weight-bearing *asanas* strengthen the bones to prevent osteoporosis from occurring in later years. In certain poses, there is a good spinal extension, which results in space being created for the regeneration of inter-vertebral discs (cartilages). Equally important, we learn to sit straight, which is a requirement not only for a normal healthy life, but also for all yoga practices.

We have thousands of miles of blood vessels and capillaries to supply blood (nourishment) to millions of cells. This wonderful 'machine' is created in such a way that it is naturally taken care of and the heart does the main job of pumping. But, it is our duty to ensure that the blood vessels and capillaries are kept clean to facilitate good circulation everywhere, even to remote areas (known as extremities). In ayurveda, *rakta shuddhi* (cleanliness of blood) is given great importance. The heart consists of muscles that need to be kept healthy by way of aerobic activities. Dynamic *yogasanas* such as Surya Namaskar cater to this need. The most effective way to maintain proper blood circulation throughout the body is by doing *asanas* and Pranayama. All the 'upside down' poses, which make use of gravity, are extremely effective in not only providing blood to all areas, but also help in the process of venous return, which rejuvenates the veins and the valves. The role played by Pranayama is on a finer level.

*Yogasanas* improve the mobility in the middle (thoracic dorsal) of the spine, thus resulting in a greater opening of the chest. This, in turn, improves the volumetric quantity of air while breathing and hence more oxygen is provided to the blood. The name given for oxygen in Sanskrit is *pranavayu*, which literally means air for vitality. *Asanas* also improve the elasticity of the diaphragm, which is responsible for inhalation and exhalation. The respiratory tract is aerodynamically designed in such a way that right at the entry point in the nostril, the inhaled air enters into the passage and into the lungs with a 'whirl effect', which reaches out to even the remote areas with increased volume to provide maximum oxygen. This principle is used by engine designers to make cylinder heads for optimum power and economy in fuel consumption. In some poses such as Sarvangasan, Setu Bandha and Halasan a partial *jalandhara bandha* (chin lock) happens on its own.

The combined positive effect of the various systems soothes and pacifies the brain and the tributaries of nerves. This helps in achieving concentration (*ekagrata*) while practising yoga. Like blood vessels, we also have hundreds of miles of nerves in our body. The spinal cord, which is an extension of the brain, is the thickest of all the nerves and is well protected in the spinal column. To achieve good physical and mental health and to go beyond into higher levels of consciousness, it is essential that these are kept clean. *Nadi shuddhi* has been given great importance in yoga. Metabolic wastes such as mucus, gas and acidity are continuously produced in the body and need to be cleansed. The *nadis,* along with the chakras, have an important role to play as high energies are diverted through them. Hatha Yoga scriptures mention these very diligently. The nervous system has to be trained as it is the carrier of impulses through the sensory and motor channels. For an uninterrupted flow of energy to pass throughout the body, it is vital that all blockages are removed to get the desired results from Pranayama.

The ductless endocrine glands are small, wonderful chemical factories that produce hormones which regulate the chemistry of our lives. An all-round *asana*-Pranayama session regulates/stimulates these glands which, in turn, work along with the nervous system to release vital hormones into the bloodstream. A classic example is the effect of poses with chin lock on the thyroid.

*Asanas* and Pranayama have a pronounced role to play for a good digestion and assimilation of the food we take. The internal muscles situated in the stomach/intestine regions function better when activated. Some *asanas* also help to drive away gases that otherwise bloat the abdomen. By not letting *vata* to stagnate, the elimination process is also eased.

It is important to keep in mind that the green signal to practise yoga during illness should come from the doctor or *vaidya* who has taken the responsibility to cure you. It has been proven that yoga and Pranayama, along with ayurveda, help to accelerate the healing process. Many institutions connected with alternative medicine are also collecting evidence to verify these positive results. A new branch in medicine, known as sports medicine, is proving very effective to cure certain illnesses, especially with regards to muscular or bone/joints-related problems. Sports medicine specialists have, in fact, adopted the movements that *asanas* provide. Basically, even during illness, the normal functioning of the body and its organs is kept up and this heals faster. However, care should be taken as each person has a different constitution. Ayurveda, combined with yoga, provides the ideal solution.

The signal given by the pain is the 'language' one has to learn to discern. During practice, one will observe a 'pleasant' pain or an 'unpleasant' pain. This holds good for the time to remain in a posture. It means one has to gradually increase the timings. But one thing is certain—in most of the cases, the relief provided is lasting and has no side-effects. For example, poses that are upside down (such as Viparita Karani) have a great effect on the mind and body, ensuring a smooth flow of *prana*, which no medicine can substitute.

The best time for yoga practice is supposed to be early morning as both the mind and body are fresh and rested. If not early morning with an empty stomach, it is advisable to start *asana* practice at least four hours after a meal or two hours after a snack or a breakfast. The traditional word for spiritual practices is known as *sandhya kaal*, twilight hours, mornings and evenings. The bowels should first be evacuated. If this has not taken place, the warming up/preparatory poses should be accompanied by upside down poses. This helps in curing constipation. Traditionally, a bath is recommended before doing any form of *puja* (prayer).

The *yogis* and sages advise that practice should be done as an offering to the Lord as a prayer, considering that the body is the temple where the soul resides. Cotton clothing is preferred as the skin 'breathes' and an overheating of the body is avoided. Tight clothing hinders movements. *Asana* practice should be done barefooted. There are so many vital pressure points in our sole which get activated as they, in turn, activate different organs in our body. The fundamental knowledge of acupressure/ acupuncture comes from ayurveda, which describes these points all over the body as *marmastanas* (sensitive points).

The *Bhagavad Gita* says that a *yogi* must avoid the two extremes of luxury and austerity. He must not fast, nor torture his flesh. He who does so cannot be a *yogi*: 'He who fasts, he who keeps awake, he who sleeps much, he who does no work, none of these can be a *yogi*.'

In poses in which you turn/twist, bend or stretch on one side, make sure to repeat each pose on each side two to three times alternately. For static types of poses, one can start with a short duration; however, the time should be gradually increased. In general, the rule is that while 'straining' one should breathe out. Do not hold the breath at any time. It results in a short supply of oxygen which, in turn, increases the body temperature and the heart rate and leads to unnecessary sweating. *Asana* practice charges your body. However, sweating will automatically happen in dynamic poses such as Surya Namaskar (where rhythmic breathing should be kept up), which is excellent not only for overall fitness, but also for aerobic activity to strengthen the heart muscles. In such cases, the preliminary warming-up phase and the cooling-down phase should always be done.

The movement of going into a pose and coming out of it should be rhythmic, graceful and confident. The deity, as well as the founder of both yoga and dance, is Shiva and there is an interconnection between the two. Yoga postures are found along with those of dance in ancient sculptures. A specialty of the type of yoga presented in this book is the judicious use of props. These are shown in the relevant photographs of the *asanas*. You may try practising with and without these props. Their goal is to lead you to the correct posture and help you to hold it for a longer period. You then achieve a better effect and avoid overstraining, which could cause injuries.

There is a tremendous choice of variations given for each pose. This helps to avoid monotony, which leads to make the posture mechanical and that is not yoga. Effort should be made during each session to explore a further range of movement with awareness. It will give you an exhilarating experience since the intent is to turn inwards.

I have also given a weekly all-round plan, based on many years of teaching experience. It is strongly recommended that you follow this to be able to understand a systematic physiological sequence of practice. Remember the age-old adage: 'no gains without pains'. Trust me, the 'gain' you will get once you make yoga a way of life is indeed beyond imagination.

# THE PRACTICE
# OF PRANAYAMA

All yoga scriptures declare that Pranayama should be practised only when you have gone through the preliminary stages of *asanas*, cleansing the internal channels (including the *nadis*), creating a stable mind, which results in correct breathing and so on. Some of them go to the extent of stating that the decision to start Pranayama rests with the guru. This is because, if *prana* is not handled properly, especially by overenthusiastic practitioners, it can do harm. It has a tremendous energy potential that needs to be handled with care. The *yogis* and masters who teach this noble art demand that before one starts practising, it is necessary to have the correct *bhavana* (attitude).

The word Pranayama is split as *prana* and *ayama*. *Prana* means vital energy or life force; *ayama* is defined as extension or expansion. Thus, Pranayama means 'extension or expansion of the dimension of *prana*'. It is a technique through which the quantity of *prana* in the body is activated to a higher frequency. Everything in this universe is a manifestation of *prana*; whatever is manifested in *stula rupa*, or 'gross form', of the subtle, cosmic energy, is *prana*. Pranayama is practised in order to understand and control the *pranic* process in the body. Breathing is a direct means of absorbing *prana* and the manner in which we breathe sets off *pranic* vibrations that influence our entire being.

According to *yogic* physiology, the human framework comprises five bodies or 'sheaths' (realms of experience), which account for the different dimensions of human existence. These are:

- *Annamaya kosha*, the food or material body
- *Manomaya kosha*, the mental body
- *Pranamaya kosha*, the vital energy body
- *Vijnanamaya kosha*, the psychic or higher mental body
- *Anandamaya kosha*, the transcendental or bliss body

These sheaths function together to form an integral whole. The practice of Pranayama, however, works mainly with *pranamaya kosha*, which, in turn, is made up of five (*pancha*) *pranas*: *prana, apana, samana, udana* and *vyana*.

*Prana* and the mind are intricately linked; the fluctuation of one means the fluctuation of the other. When either the mind or *prana* becomes balanced, the other is steadied. By being aware of the nature of the breath and by restraining it, the whole system gets controlled. When you retain the breath, you are stopping nervous impulses in different parts of the body and are harmonising the brainwave patterns. In Pranayama, it is the duration of breath retention that has to increase. The longer the breath is held, the greater the gap between nervous impulses and their responses in the brain. This is not recommended for beginners as the process has to be gradually learnt and practised.

Patanjali defines Pranayama as the gap between inhalation and exhalation. Pranayama is usually considered to be the practice of controlled inhalation and exhalation combined with retention. Actually, retention (*kumbhaka*) allows a longer period for the assimilation of

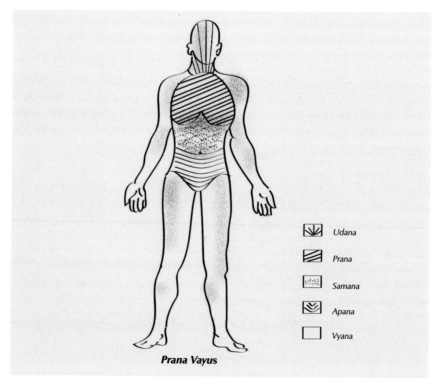

Udana

Prana

Samana

Apana

Vyana

**Prana Vayus**

*The pranic body*

*prana*, just as it allows more time for the exchange of gases (oxygen and carbon dioxide) in the cells. This interesting interplay of the mind and the *prana* has been a subject of great introspection by various spiritual systems down the centuries. An ardent student of yoga is expected to take up the challenge of experimenting, exploring and experiencing these phenomena within. Then only can the student break all barriers to explore the inner cosmos and come closer to realising the 'self'. Becoming introverted is the first step.

Pranayamas such as *Nadi Shodhan (Anulom-Vilom)*, *Kapalbhati* and *Agnisar* belong to the 'dynamic' category and they contribute immensely to the internal cleansing of the channels, activating the digestive system along with the internal organs and clearing up the nasal passage and the lungs. This leads to not only a healthy mind and body but also cures innumerable ailments that afflict people of all age groups. For practical purpose one can name these Pranayamas as the 'Dynamic set' and the other simple Pranayamas as the 'Static set'. The latter are chiefly 'mind-oriented'; the main purpose being to achieve *prana* connectivity, which leads the practitioner, step by step, to higher states (meditative) of consciousness.

To help this process further, it is recommended that you chant 'Om' at least eight times initially while exhaling in Ujjayi Pranayama. 'Om' is greatly misunderstood as a religious symbol. The vibration created by the correct chanting of this mantra, which is known as *pranava*, elevates the mind to the highest state (the fourth), known as *turyaawasta* (the ultimate state of consciousness). It takes you beyond the other three states of dream (*swapna*), awake (*jagrut*) and dreamless sleep (*sushupti*).

Concentrated Pranayama practice, with faith, prepares you to achieve this state in due course. Even as one begins to practise, a 'glimpse' of super consciousness is experienced.

In my classes and workshops, I generally play the *tanpura* on a music recording as accompaniment to the mantra, which I download online (there are useful mobile apps available for this). The pitch needs to be selected, as it varies from person to person. The idea is to 'merge' one's chant with the vibrations of the *tanpura*. The participants are totally amazed at the outcome and later tell me that they have never experienced anything as divine.

It is to be remembered that this book of guidelines is for the 'common person'. Keeping this in mind, I have tried to keep all the *asanas* and Pranayama simple and easy to practise, giving an understanding of their background as well. The intent is to motivate you to perform your household and other duties better, with improved concentration, with a calm mind and, at the same time, guide you to travel the path of spiritualism through yoga.

The timing and preconditions for Pranayama practice are similar to those mentioned for *asanas*. Pranayama can be done after *asana* practice or separately, depending on the time available. The best results are achieved after a short duration of resting/recovery poses. Beginners should first learn breath awareness. You should observe the natural (without interference) breath, its velocity, timing and depth all the way to the pelvic region. This can then be compared during the inhalation and exhalation stages. You will notice that it is not the same. These observations are very helpful as they make it easier for the later stages of Pranayama practice. The posture can initially be chosen as supine or leaning against the wall or bed, in Sukhasan or Veerasan.

Ideally, one is expected to switch over from supine to sitting to keep the spine firmly erect, which, in turn, keeps the mind sharp. The ribcage remains in its place and does not drop during exhalations. Incidentally, even while learning Indian classical music, the teachers insist on keeping the spine erect, without leaning against anything.

### The 'Dynamic' Set

- *Nadi Shodhan* (purify) also known as *Anulom-Vilom* (alternate nostril breathing): Closing the eyes will help in better concentration. Close the right nostril with the right-hand thumb and breathe gently through the left nostril. When the lungs are full, breathe out from the right nostril by closing the left with the middle and third fingers. Then inhale this time from the right nostril and exhale from the left. Continue this alternatively for a few minutes. You can also take breaks in between.

I have not explained the advantages of this method as I strongly believe that the practitioner himself 'explores' and finds out what good it does to him. This is a 'subjective' science. Each time you practise, you will realise that it brings a whole new experience to the mind and the body. Otherwise, monotonous repetitions make it boring. You should keep on changing the ratios of inhalation and exhalation. The fundamental idea is to balance the right and the left lobes of the brain as this ultimately affects the functions in the mind. Predominance of one will be corrected. The practitioner will note that, to begin with, both sides of the nostrils will not be the same.

- *Kapalbhati* (cleansing of frontal brain, forehead) is the sixth of the *shat karmas* mentioned in the Hatha Yoga scriptures. This Pranayama is most popular owing to its propagation by Swami Ramdev. Its practice leads to several advantages, including the cure of various diseases as it invigorates the entire brain as well as awakens the dormant centres within the body. The *shloka* (verse) describing it in Hatha Yoga text mentions that the breathing should be done like the pumping action of a pair of bellows (of a blacksmith).

Sit in Siddhasan or Veerasan or stand in Utkatasan (as shown in the section on Preparatory *Asanas*), inhale deeply. Do the respirations in quick succession with both nostrils simultaneously. Initially you can do it 25 times at a stretch and, in due course, you can increase it to a hundred, laying emphasis on fast exhalations. Let the inhalations happen on their own. In the beginning, it is advisable to take a small break in between to avoid dizziness. Here, too, you should keep the spine firmly erect with the ribcage lifted (jacked) up. The movement is only in the diaphragm.

- *Agnisara Kriya*: As the name suggests, this *kriya* (activity, dynamic *yogic* practice) creates 'fire' in the centre of the body (*sara*, essence) where the abdominal muscles and organs are located. *Agnisara* takes care of this and removes (burns out) excessive *kapha* from the system. Digestion improves and, along with it, the extra accumulated fat also disappears. It awakens all the systems from within, thus fulfilling the goal of also cleansing the blood vessels and its fine tributaries (the capillaries) and enables *prana* to flow easily.

After selecting a sitting or a standing (Utkatasan) posture, exhale fully (*bahya kumbhaka*) and pull the stomach/abdomen inside in quick succession for five/seven times without breathing in. Then gently breathe in normally. This cycle should be repeated a few times initially and, later, you can go up to 15-20 times of withdrawing the abdomen during one cycle. How much you should do is left to your discretion, but a firm goal should be set up before the start. At the end of these Pranayamas it is advised to lie in Savasan for some time. Within a few minutes of doing these Pranayamas, I have seen people removing their woollens, in spite of the cold temperature in the room. Precaution should be taken by those who have high blood pressure, intestinal problems or excessive *pitta*.

## The 'Static' Set

- *Ujjayi* Pranayama: This is the simplest of all Pranayamas and can be done in any comfortable position, even Savasan. *Ujjayi* means to conquer or acquire by conquest. Here, a sort of meditation happens on its own as your concentration becomes deep and intense. Exhale fully in the beginning and then take a deep, long inhalation until the lungs are full. During this breathing, a hissing/snoring sound from the throat is expected. The exhalation and inhalation should be done only through the nostrils. The breath is not held back. During the natural exhalation, care is to be taken to not allow the ribcage to drop. After one or two cycles, do natural breathing without controlling, just observing. Once again start the *Ujjayi* cycle.

  A variation is to keep the head in *jalandhara bandha* (chin lock) position. This Pranayama can also be done while chanting 'Om' during exhalation. Basically there is no time limit set, but it should be regularly practised for at least 10 to 15 minutes. Great emphasis is laid on the phase between inhalation and exhalation. There is no holding the breath or specific concentration involved but a kind of observation (called *sahaja*, the natural state) takes one to an elevated and timeless state of meditation. Meditation just happens. This comes with practise and can be done in any comfortable posture. Practise, practise and practise is the key to achieving this state. The *bhavana* (attitude, faith) with which you practise also plays a very important role.

- *Viloma* Pranayama: *Viloma* means against the natural order of things as inhalation and exhalation is interrupted and done in stages with various permutations and combinations. It is best done after a preliminary round of *Ujjayi*. Here, too, a comfortable posture can be selected as long as the upper body can be kept active and the chest and abdomen region are 'open' to be able to utilise the maximum volume that the system can allow.

Version One: After exhaling fully, inhale in two equally divided stages and, when the lungs are full, exhale deeply without any interruption. This is one cycle.

Version Two: After exhaling fully, inhale without interruption and exhale in two equally divided stages. This is one cycle.

Version Three: Inhale and exhale in two equally divided stages each. This forms one cycle.

After each cycle, it is advisable to do one or two cycles of normal breathing. This is equivalent to 'calibrating' an instrument, each time before using it, to check the zero level. Each version can be done a couple of times and you can shift to different permutations and combinations of the stages of interruptions—two, three, four and so on. This technique has the advantage that it can never be mechanical as one is kept mentally active. It increases the sensitivity within our subtle *pranic* system.

- *Kumbhaka* (retention): According to the *Hatha Yoga Pradipika*, 'By stopping the *prana* through retention, the mind becomes free from all modifications. By thus practising (*Kumbhaka*) one achieves the stage of Raja Yoga (supreme union).' This quote is mentioned with the intention to show the importance of *Kumbhaka* in practice. Many variations are mentioned in the texts, but we shall deal with only two of them—*Antara Kumbhaka* (retention after full inhalation) and *Bahya Kumbhaka* (retention after full exhalation).

  *Antara Kumbhaka* after *puraka* (inhalation): Sit with the spine erect. Exhale fully and then inhale deeply (*ujjayi*), followed by a short pause to do a chin lock. Retain the breath for a few seconds. Initially, the retention should not be too long. Gently release the chin lock before exhaling. Do one or two normal breathing cycles to resume.

  *Bahya Kumbhaka* after *rechaka* (exhalation): Follow the same instructions as above with the exception that the retention will be after full exhalation. Care should be taken to ensure that you do not overdo these *kumbhakas*, which could result in heaviness in the head. Those with high blood pressure should not practise these.

At the end of Pranayama, it is best to lie down in Savasan and let the positive (*sattvic*) after-effects of the practice take over the mind.

# YOGA THERAPY
# FOR AILMENTS

The basic purpose of yoga is to take one beyond our 'normal' life to higher levels of spiritualism, which obviously demands an immense amount of effort. Yoga is the science of physical and mental harmony. Fortunately for us, the 'roadmap' has been delineated by our ancient yogis and rishis. In the process, they also developed methods to get rid of diseases or disorders of all kinds, which would have otherwise served as obstacles on the path. Their asana and Pranayama practices helped them to understand the human body and the mind in different (at times very extreme) conditions. They used their intelligence with perseverance to correlate with nature. This is how they researched, developed and practised the great science of yoga and ayurveda. At the same time, they discovered the potential healing abilities of the mind and the body. Asana and Pranayama practice aids this process. Keeping the doshas well balanced with a regimented daily routine is of vital importance in curing various ailments.

Three decades ago, we, as yoga teachers, had to deal with people who wanted to learn yoga only to 'cure' them of their problems. We soon learnt from our master to develop the attitude that behind every 'patient' there is a spiritual aspirant and accept the challenge to teach them and win them over and hence take them further into the spiritual domain of life. Later, many admitted that it was a blessing in disguise that took them to yoga. Yoga teachers took up the challenge to inform themselves of all levels of medical sciences and diseases or ailments and, of course, ayurveda. We came to understand a fascinating new branch of medicine, known as sports medicine, which has a different approach to understanding the science of movements in the human body while it is in the process of rigorous preparations to win medals in competitions. It also had to take care of injuries and hence developed an ideal process of 'recovery' and 'repair'.

While teaching, we made sure that the flag of yoga was kept flying high so that we did not bring disrepute to it or to ayurveda. In addition, we kept up our own practice to be able to search and research the 'inner world'.

For example, I have also done all the *pancha karma*s under guidance to understand and appreciate the 'wonders' of balancing the *dosha*s, along with internal cleansing. Giving tips on health, as mentioned and practised in ayurveda, to my students also helped in getting rid of their problems/ailments and, at the same time, brought harmony into their lives.

Having an ailment means that one particular organ or part of the body has a problem. This can also have side-effects that affect other organs or parts within the body. Once the root cause is diagnosed, one should keep the other systems 'healthy' and working properly. This helps the diseased system to cure much faster. It should be emphasised here that the diagnosis of a disturbed *dosha* in ayurveda is most effective as it works not only to cure it in the due course of time, but it also arrests further deterioration almost immediately. We should not get discouraged by an ailment and get depressed. Instead, consider it a challenge; view it as a 'blessing in disguise'.

In this book, I have taken up three health problems that many are suffering from these days—knee pain; lower back pain (lumbar spine) and neck/shoulder (cervical spine) stiffness and/or pain. In all the three cases, pain is understood to be arising from the wear and tear in the concerned joints (popularly known as spondylitis) and not from injuries or ligament tears arising out of accidents or from muscle fatigue. This has to first be established by either an X-ray or MRI investigation.

According to ayurveda, in all these three cases, the wear and tear is caused by the *dosha* known as vata, whose quality is 'cold' and 'drying'. Irrespective of your predominant *dosha*, vata, with its drying quality, increases with age. We know from experience that as age advances, the 'cracking noise' in the joints, dryness in the skin and hair, flatulence in the afternoons (*vata* period) and the beginning of dryness in the stool increase. This is a natural and slow process but its effects are far more if we live a sedentary lifestyle and do not move our bodies (joints and muscles) sufficiently.

The other quality of *vata* is also that which 'moves' (its job is to carry nutrition, fluids and so on to different parts of the body) in the system. But, when it 'sits', its negative effects are faster and dries up the fluid (lubricating) in the joints.

The 'seat' of vata is the large intestine. Not to allow the digested material (faeces) to 'settle' down for a longer time is the best way to avoid vata generation. That is why in our culture it has been a practice to empty the large intestine very early in the morning. The other reason is, of course, food. There are certain kinds of food that contribute to increased vata formation much before reaching the large intestine. In India, tadka (tempering of mustard seeds, turmeric, jeera and other spices in oil) are added to cooked lentils to avoid this effect and, at the same time, to help digestion (agni) to get maximum nutrition (better assimilation). Another item that is extremely popular in our culture is ghee (clarified butter). When a diya (lamp) is lit during puja, its combustion is very clear in comparison to other oils. The same thing happens during the digestion process. Ghee's viscosity at body temperature is also conducive to our system as it protects the inner linings exceptionally well. It is an excellent antidote to disturbed vata in the system as it prevents the 'drying up' process.

Keeping the body warm and exercising regularly also keeps vata away. I remember that, on weekends, drops of til (sesame) oil were put in my nose and ears before going to sleep. At the same time, once a week, castor oil (sometimes medicated) was given to me with warm water before going to sleep.

In yoga, there are many types of asanas that keep our natural movements intact by providing all-round mobility to the joints. Besides the joints, other tissues, muscles, ligaments and so on should also be taken care of. The large 'organ', the skin, also needs to be kept active by not allowing the drying process of vata to take charge. Massaging the skin and hair works wonders here. Doing yogasanas to keep mobility in the joints and help them to perform their functions properly by maintaining muscle tone is highly recommended. But, it is expected from the practitioner to use his discretion and 'listen' to the body, which will act and react by 'talking' to you. It will tell you when you make a movement that is not favourable. Please do not take a painkiller as it has a 'deafening' effect when the body 'talks'.

Go ahead with your yoga practice with full faith and enthusiasm; you can follow the weekly timetable I have prepared in practising the asanas. Make sure to use the props that are mentioned in the pages as 'variations' and also as shown in the photographs. This is the strength of this yoga system. Gradually increase your timings; that is, the number of breaths. Immediately come out of a pose if you get a 'negative' pain. Please do not use force.

**Suggested *Asanas***

- Knee: Poses that stretch the calves (Parshvottanasan); strengthen the quadriceps (Utkatasan); lying down hamstring stretch (Supta Padangustasan) and standing poses with the support of a wall. The *asanas* will bring back the balance of these muscle groups. Sit in Veerasan or Baddhakonasan with props. This helps in bringing back the lost movement that was provided by nature. It also provides for better blood and *prana* flow in the joint. Do not sit on the floor with crossed legs (Sukhasan). It is 'poison' for the knee joint at this state until the pain subsides. The inverted poses are excellent for recovery and good blood circulation and for your well-being in general. All kinds of jerks are to be avoided. That means no jogging for the time being. Reducing the body weight also helps in decreasing the load on the knee cartilages.

- Lower spine: Here, the main precaution is that you should not have severe pain in or along the sciatica nerve, which goes all the way down to the heel. If that is the case, then you should follow the advice of a physiotherapist to relieve this pain. Even otherwise, bending forward with straight legs, lifting weights, sitting for too long in one position, and so on, should be totally avoided.

  All standing poses, as shown in the 'variations', can be done for a short duration to strengthen and tone the complete anatomy, followed by Supta Padangustasan. All forms of twisting are very effective. No forward bending, but simple back bends with props and support (as shown in Adhomukha Swanasan) would prove beneficial. Adhomukha Vrksasan on a door frame and Prasarita Padottanasan (with two chairs) would give an instant relief. Being aware of the correct sitting posture at all times is imperative.

- Neck/shoulder region, cervical spine: Here, too, an X-ray or MRI should determine the extent of the problem. If not in the cervical part of the spine, then, the lopsided 'load' of the head (which weighs about two-and-a-half kilograms) at a wrong angle for prolonged time, sometimes for years at a stretch, has resulted in stiffness owing to fatigue in the concerned muscle groups. Caution is to be exercised if there is a problem of compression in the cervical disc, in which case you should only follow the doctor's advice. There are also certain types of sports and exercise regimens such as improper weight training while working out in a fitness studio that build unnatural and unwanted stiffness in this region. This results in an imbalance of muscles and tissues and has a devastating effect in the long run.

All poses shown in the section, 'Preparatory Poses', which are marked as 'variations', will provide immediate relief. For an all-round effect, all the other poses can be worked out as shown in the Suggested Weekly Plan. Sirsasan, Sarvangasan and Halasan can be avoided initially or as long as the pain persists. If there is an improvement, you can try out the ones shown as 'variations' and using props (bolsters) at short intervals.

Pranayamas, both Static and Dynamic, should be regularly practised by all. The postures can be selected as per your capacity to stay for sometime without disturbance. They will definitely prove to be extremely beneficial and contribute to your well-being.

# WEEKLY PLAN FOR THE PRACTICE OF *ASANAS/* PRANAYAMA

It is important that a proper method of warming up, cooling down and adhering to the correct sequences is followed. With this in mind, a weekly plan has been 'designed' to suit everyone in general so that maximum benefit can be achieved.

## Monday

| | |
|---|---|
| Preparatory | 10 minutes |
| Standing | 30 minutes |
| Recovery | 10 minutes |
| Inverted | 20 minutes |
| Pranayama | 15 minutes |

## Tuesday

| | |
|---|---|
| Preparatory | 10 minutes |
| Back Bends | 20 minutes |
| Recovery | 10 minutes |
| Standing | 20 minutes |
| Inverted | 20 minutes |
| Pranayama | 05 minutes |

## Wednesday

| | |
|---|---|
| Preparatory | 10 minutes |
| Surya Namaskar | 10 minutes |
| Standing | 15 minutes |
| Recovery | 10 minutes |
| Inverted | 20 minutes |
| Pranayama | 15 minutes |

## Thursday

| | |
|---|---|
| Twisting | 06 minutes |
| Standing | 05 minutes |
| Preparatory | 15 minutes |
| Forward Bends | 40 minutes |
| Abs/Balancing | 15 minutes |
| Inverted | 20 minutes |

## Friday

| | |
|---|---|
| Preparatory | 15 minutes |
| Standing | 45 minutes |
| Recovery | 05 minutes |
| Twisting | 10 minutes |
| Inverted | 20 minutes |
| Pranayama | 15 minutes |

## Sunday

| | |
|---|---|
| Twisting | 05 minutes |
| Preparatory | 10 minutes |
| Surya Namaskar | 10 minutes |
| | (no break) |
| Back Bends | 20 minutes |
| Inverted | 20 minutes |
| Pranayama | 15 minutes |

These are broad guidelines for a good all-round practice. In the process of following these, you will gradually understand the logic behind this weekly plan and the variety it offers. It is of utmost importance that this concept of variety is kept up. Otherwise, one practises 'mechanically', with the result that the mind, true to its inherent nature, wanders off. It should keep you focused and guessing as to what feedback you are getting this time with this variation and so on. Then only is it yoga practice in the true sense.

Later, you can make changes to the order, deciding on a system that suits you the most. Be careful, do not fall in the trap of doing only those poses that you like because they are easy and comfortable. You also have props at your disposal to help you stay longer in the poses and get the maximum benefit, both, at physiological and mental levels (without injuries or damages). Saturday has been left out as a holiday; it can be any other day. Once you get to practise a few times, you can change the sequences and/or the timings. This self-practise (*sadhana*) will ultimately give you confidence and motivate you further.

Pranayama should also be done during your regular practice. I suggest that you do not 'blindly' follow what is being mentioned here; instead, question it and try it out with an attitude of *jignyasa* (curiosity). You will then automatically go deeper into the subject, which is 'you' in this case!

# PREPARATORY &
# INTERMEDIATE POSES

**Tadasan**
*(stay for 25 breaths)*

**Adhomukha Svanasan**
*(stay for 40 breaths)*

**Vrkshasan**
*(stay for 25 breaths)*

**Adhomukha Vrkshasan**
*(stay for 15 breaths)*

**Utkatasan**
*(stay for 25 breaths)*

**Utthita Hasta Padangushtasan**
*(stay for 25 breaths each side)*

**Uttanasan**
*(stay for 25 breaths)*

**Supta Padangushtasan**
*(stay for 25 breaths each side)*

Any form of exercises or *asanas* needs 'warming up' of the required muscle groups, joints, organs and so on by facilitating the blood circulation so that you can easily stretch or contract the various muscles and limbs of the body. This results in greater flexibility and better coordination as a preparation for the required posture or movement. These poses also help you to position and program your body and limbs to understand your anatomy. For, if it is not in tune with nature, you will get a 'signal' with a 'not good' pain. You will then make changes and try to achieve adequate 'realignment'.

Your process of 'internalising' has just begun; you are on the path to yoga. Keep your breathing *sahaj* (normal).

# TADASAN

We spend hours standing but never give a thought as to whether we stand correctly. A wrong way of standing leads to one-sided pressure on the cartilages of the joints of the lower back, hips and knees. Tadasan teaches us to stand properly and, with practice, it improves our posture. This *asana* is the foundation for the standing poses. Experience the steadiness in the mind that comes with it.

Eyes fixed
on one spot

Neck relaxed

Forearms
turned inwards

Arms turned
outwards

Knee caps
pulled up

Knee caps
pulled up

Shoulders
back

Spine
raised up

Buttocks in

Back of
legs stretched

# VRKSHASAN

Learning to stand in Vrkshasan improves steadiness and it gives a sense of balance and poise to the body. The stretching of the arms helps in lifting the spine; it also relieves stiffness in the neck and shoulders.

Sides stretched up

Knees back

Knee caps pulled up

# UTKATASAN

Utkatasan strengthens the ankles, thighs and calf muscles. The spine is lifted up, the chest is expanded. This helps in relieving tension in the neck and shoulders. It also strengthens the peripheral muscles such as the quadriceps around the knee joint.

## For Beginners

Back to
the wall

Sides stretched up

Buttocks as if sitting

Heels pressed down

# UTTANASAN

This pose stretches the upper back as it relieves stiffness in the lower back and neck/shoulder region. The folded hands, when pulled towards the floor, stretch the sides of the chest. As one stays in the pose, there is a tremendous pull in the back of the knee region (hamstring muscles). You should not be afraid of the temporary pain that accompanies the stretch. The hamstring muscles are quite strong and play a very important role for the legs, knees and the lower spine. Since the level of the head is below that of the heart and the diaphragm is stretched, it forms an excellent recovery pose in between, while doing strenuous *asanas* such as the standing poses. Feet on brick stretches the calf muscles, which, in turn, help to tone the 'auxiliary pump' to the heart.

## Commencing Pose

Sides of chest stretched down

Arms stretched down with palms

Knee caps pulled up

Thighs turned out

Back of legs stretched

Arches opened

Feet kept parallel

Body weight transferred towards front feet

# Variations

Feet on brick

One leg in Padmasan

Palms under feet

Twist sideways

Groins resting on chair

# ADHOMUKHA SVANASAN

Like Uttanasan, it also stretches the calves, hamstrings, the complete spine (both posterior and anterior), hands and shoulders. In the process of stretching, it relieves the stiffness of various joints. This pose is also a preparatory pose to Sirsasan and helps in recovery if done for 5 to 10 minutes with support. The diaphragm takes in more volume of air in inhalation and thus reduces the pressure on the heart. It tones up the digestive system and helps in getting rid of gases from the intestines. This is a very versatile pose as it is beneficial to do at any stage of *yogasana* practice.

Neck relaxed

Elbows locked

Knee caps pulled up

Back of legs stretched

Feet parallel

Bottom soles stretched

Heels pressed down

## Variations

Hands on chair

Thumbs and fingers pressed against the wall

# ADHOMUKHA VRKSHASAN

This pose releases tension and builds up strength in the neck, shoulder, arms and wrists. The blood circulation to the areas also improves. It makes you stretch your spine, which gets toned as preparation for other *asanas*.

## Commencing Pose

Jump, with back to wall

## Variations

## Variations

Heels stretched

Neck relaxed

Elbows locked

At the door frame

Strap on elbow

# UTTHITA HASTA PADANGUSHTASAN

This pose works on very important muscles, the hamstrings, as mentioned in Uttanasan. The complete anatomy, from the hip to the ankles, is realigned, removing stiffness in the hip joint. If adequate time is given for the practice of this pose, the other subsequent *asanas* in the standing poses and forward bends will become easier. People with pain in the lower spine (lumbar) and knees must practise this pose regularly.

Hip turned outward

Thigh turned outward

Back of leg, heel, stretched

Knee cap pulled up

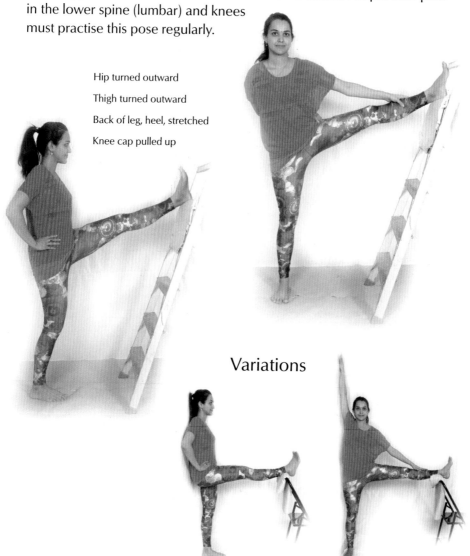

## Variations

# SUPTA PADANGUSHTASAN

Back of leg, heel stretched

To the side

## Variation

Using strap

# SURYA NAMASKAR

This is a very popular Dynamic *asana* series and it is a beneficial all-round form of exercise. Some people believe that by doing this regularly, you do not need to practise other *asana*s. This is true if one performs 108 cycles!

Namaskarasan    →    Urdhva Hastasan    →    Uttanasan    →

Namaskarasan    ←    Urdhva Hastasan    ←    Uttanasan    ←

Surya Namaskar is not a substitute for a full *asana* programme, which is needed for an all-round effect on the body and the mind from the point of view of yoga. Like any other form of exercise, here, too, warming up (with poses from the Preparatory Section) and cooling down (with Recovery poses) is absolutely necessary. The number of cycles can be increased gradually. You can continue with any other set of *asana*s. Maintaining rhythmic breathing and rhythmic movements is suggested.

Walk or jump back    Adhomukhasvanasan    ⟶    Urdhva Mukhasvanasan

Chaturangadandasan

Walk or jump forward    Adhomukhasvanasan    ⟵    Urdhva Mukhasvanasan

# STANDING POSES

**Trikonasan**

**Parshva Konasan**

**Ardha Chandrasan**

**Parivritta Trikonasan**

**Parivritta Parshvakonasan**

**Veerbhadrasan**

**Parshvottanasan**

**Prasarita Padottanasan**

This set of poses stretch, strengthen and activate all the different joints and parts of the body. In the process, they also 'realign' the complete anatomy, while removing the muscular imbalances that result due to improper (unnatural) movement, wrong habits and one-sided activities (for example, from certain sports). These poses prepare you to withstand, with ease, various activities in daily life and also be able to perform different *asanas* of forward, backwards, twistings or upside-down nature. They have proved very useful all over the world, even for extreme sports or athletic activities and are the speciality of the Iyengar system of yoga.

To start with, it is advisable to do these poses by using the support of a wall, as shown in the subsequent pages. It is best to stay for about one minute (25 breaths) each side and repeat the cycle twice.

# TRIKONASAN

To look at this pose seems simple, but the dynamism accompanied by the vibrancy, which it displays within, is worth experiencing. While repeating the pose in the variations shown in the pictures, you will discover a new experience each time. Through the activation in various muscle groups such as hamstrings, quadriceps (above the knee), ankles, calfs, hip joints, spine, shoulders and neck region, you will feel that a firm foundation is being laid for the body. This pose not only strengthens but also realigns the body back to its natural anatomical position.

## Commencing Poses

Distance between feet should be one leg length

## Variations

Elbow locked

Arms turned outwards

Hip turned

Head turned up

Thigh turned outwards

Knee cap pulled up

Leaning back against the wall

Hands on the wall, fingers facing down, foot on the wall

# PARSHVA KONASAN

The lower part of the body below the pelvis remains the same as the previous pose. But the upper back undergoes a good 'awakening' through the side stretch of the spine. The sides of the hips are also well stretched to prevent the formation of excess fat.

## Commencing Poses

Distance between feet should be one-and-a-half leg length

Elbow locked

Chest turned to the side

Thigh revolved outwards

Knee back-pressing upper arm

Knee in line with heel to form a 90 degree angle

## Variations

Hands on the wall, fingers facing down

Leaning back against the wall

# ARDHA CHANDRASAN

As the weight is shifted to one leg, it strengthens its muscles as well as the hip and knee joints. It is one of the best poses to remove hip stiffness. Along with the stretch, the lower back also gets relief.

## Commencing Poses

Distance between feet should be one-and-a-half leg length

Bend front leg to move hand forward and continue

## Variations

Leaning back against the wall

Arm turned outwards

Thigh revolved outward

Lift

Stretch

Finger tips pressed on floor

Hands on the wall, fingers facing down

# PARIVRITTA TRIKONASAN

These poses give a wonderful lateral twist to the complete spine, along with the active participation of its connected muscles of the legs, buttocks, the front and back of the chest, shoulders and hands. Stiffness in the spine is released and the spinal muscles are strengthened. The abdominal organs in this region also get toned.

## Commencing Poses

Distance between feet should be one leg length

Upper body turned

## Variations

Begin by facing the wall, then lean back against it

Hand stretched up

Side chest revolved

Back leg extended

Foot turned inwards

Hands on the wall, fingers facing down

# PARIVRITTA PARSHVAKONASAN

## Commencing Poses

Distance between feet should be one-and-a-half leg length

Upper body turned

Elbow locked

Chest turned up sideways

Thigh revolved

## Variations

Hands on the wall, fingers facing down

Leaning back against the wall

# VEERBHADRASAN

Not only is this pose named after a warrior, but it also makes you feel like one. With the legs firm on the floor and the chest expanded further through a stretch in the arms to allow deep breathing, the body is charged with energy. It gives firmness to the body as it strengthens the legs and the lower back.

## Commencing Poses

Distance between feet should be one-and-a-half leg length

Sides of chest pulled upwards

Hip socket in

Heel stretched

Knee in line with heel to form a 90 degree angle

Heel pressed, sole extended

Revolve to make knee face floor

## Variation

# Commencing Poses

Buttocks kept in level

Look at fingers

Stretch

# Variation

# PARSHVOTTANASAN

This pose has the same benefits of Uttanasan. With full extension of the back leg, the spine can be further extended on the side. The folded palms/hands behind give relief to the neck, shoulder and wrists. It also strengthens the vital hamstring muscles and calfs. There is a realignment of the hip joint.

## Commencing Pose

Hands joined or folded

Elbows up

Buttock in same line

Thigh revolved inwards

Back leg extended

Back foot in

Heel pressed on floor

## Variations

Hands on the wall

Hands extended to the floor

# PRASARITA PADOTTANASAN

This is a variation of Uttanasan; however, here, the legs are spread. The stretch of the hamstring muscles and those connected with the lower spine are stretched further. Stiffness or pain in the hips is relieved. The advantages of Uttanasan with regards to the heart, digestion, relief to neck and shoulder are also there in this pose.

Outer edges of feet pressed

## Variations

Hands on the wall

# RECOVERY POSES

**Dandasan**

**Gomukhasan**

**Veerasan**

**Supta Veerasan**

**Baddhakonasan**

**Supta Baddhakonasan**

**Padmasan**

**Matsyasan**

Any form of physical activity, be it in daily life or while exercising, results in strain, stressing our systems at various levels. This includes the 'load' on the heart muscles that have to cater to the demand for a higher need of oxygen to be supplied to the body. The uniqueness of *yogasanas* lies in fulfilling these requirements to their maximum, resulting in a quick 'recharge' as the chest 'opening' provides for a greater volume of oxygen for breathing.

The postures given here, when combined with those in the section of 'Preparatory/Intermediate Poses', can best serve this purpose. Moreover, the overuse of certain muscles and joints that create imbalance will be 'neutralised' immediately. In sports medicine terminology, the lactic acid that has gone beyond its specified limits can be kept under control by practising these simple but very effective poses. *Ujjai* breathing will certainly help the recovery process of the body and calm the mind. It is best to stay for about 5 to 10 minutes on each side.

# DANDASAN

Just like Tadasan in standings poses, Dandasan is the foundation for seated postures. It teaches you to sit upright without stooping or dropping the shoulders. The stretching and alignment of the legs and feet, right from the hips to the toes, should be done, as it will form the basis for twistings or forward bends with one or both legs attached.

Chest/spine raised up
Arms turned outwards
Abdomen soft

Knee cap pulled
Back of legs, heel extended
Palm pressed on floor

# GOMUKHASAN

This posture removes stiffness in the hip joint, ankles, shoulders, neck, wrists and fingers. Stay for 25 breaths each side and repeat.

## Variation

# VEERASAN

The warriors (*veer*) in earlier times used to sit in the courts of the kings in this pose as it also allowed them to quickly get up, if required. Hence the name 'Veerasan'. This is one of the best recovery poses as it gives a good 'rest' to the legs if you have been standing for a long time, walked, cycled or played games or done standing poses. Make it a habit of sitting in this pose while doing other things. The ankles, knees, hips get 'realigned' and will spare you from problems of these joints. If you already have joint problems, then it should be done with the help of props, as shown in the photographs. This will not only relieve the pain but will also stop further deterioration. It is also a good pose for Pranayama.

## Variation

# SUPTA VEERASAN

This is an extension of the sitting version with the spine rested and the abdomen/diaphragm stretched, thus the volume of breath increases and the recovery is faster. It can be done even after eating. End this pose by bending forward, if required.

Press down

Reduce this gap        Stretch

## Variations

# BADDHAKONASAN

A sedentary lifestyle restricts our movement in the hip and knee joints and results in several ailments. This *asana* not only helps to regain the knee and hip movement but also cures pelvic- and abdomen-related ailments. It is also very beneficial for women.

Soles pressed against each other

# SUPTA BADDHAKONASAN

This is a continuation of the sitting version and can also be done after eating. It gets rid of gases and, with the spine rested, it stretches the sides of the pelvis to facilitate deeper breathing and better blood circulation in the region. It also gives relief to lower back pain.

Buttocks on edge of support

# PADMASAN

Who does not want to pose in Padmasan and look like a *yogi*? Many Pranayamas and meditations are practised in this pose, according to *yogic* scriptures. But they do not reveal that it is only in this pose that you can achieve *moksha*.

I have seen many people who have permanently injured their knees trying to forcefully do this pose. It is remarkable how a retired general managed to keep his knees and legs 'intact', despite the rigorous exercises which he carried out during the tenure in the army. The secret is that he kept sitting cross-legged whenever he could. This *asana* comes easily only to those who sit cross-legged on the floor. Practising Veerasan and Badhakonasan helps to regain the mobility in the ankles, knees and hip joint. You can gradually try with one leg at a time. It is also advisable to alternate the leg positions while sitting for a longer duration in Padmasan.

## Commencing Pose

## Variations

Bending forward on stomach

Bending forward

# MATSYASAN

This pose gives a stretch to the pelvis, abdominal or diaphragmic muscles and also to the complete spine. This is a vital region of the body that requires toning.

## Commencing Pose

# TWISTINGS

**Pashasan**

**Ardha Matsyendrasan**

**Bharadvajasan**

**Marichyasan**

Actually, Twistings also fall under the category of Recovery Poses. In the present day of sedentary lifestyles, people tend to sit on chairs and sofas, which, in turn, make their bodies 'sluggish'. Many work in offices and sit at the table for long hours with an incorrect posture, leading to overstraining, thus stiffening the neck/shoulder and the lower back region. This has resulted in consequential ailments such as headaches, sciatica and the weakening of the spinal muscles. Twistings not only help avoid these problems, but also strengthen the peripheral spinal muscles, which keep the spine erect and allow an easy flow of breathing in the pelvic region.

It is suggested that every one hour, a break should be given at the workplace to release the collected tension. You can do these poses with the help of a chair. The complete spine undergoes a good lateral twist brought about by the hands acting as leverages. The muscles and organs situated in the abdomen region get activated due to the internal 'massage'. During the twist process, one should breathe out. A stay (with normal breathing ) in the pose of about 40 seconds (20 breaths) each side should suffice for good results. Each cycle can be repeated two to three times.

# PASHASAN

### Back View

Shoulder back

# ARDHA MATSYENDRASAN

### Variation

Holding wrist from behind

# BHARADVAJASAN

## Back View

## Variation

On chair

# MARICHYASAN

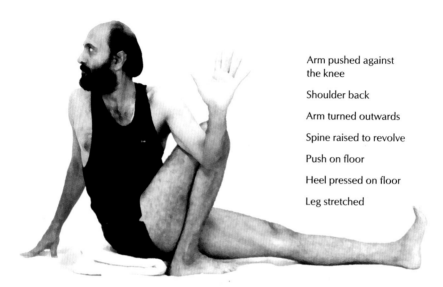

Arm pushed against
the knee

Shoulder back

Arm turned outwards

Spine raised to revolve

Push on floor

Heel pressed on floor

Leg stretched

## Back View

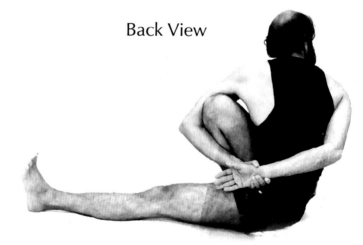

## Variation

Hands on wall

# FORWARD BENDS

**Janu Sirshasan**

**Parivritta Janu Sirshasan**

**Triang Mukhaekapada Paschimottanasan**

**Ardha Baddha Padma Paschimottanasan**

**Upavishta Konasan**

**Parshva Upavishta Konasan**

**Krounchasan**

**Paschimottanasan**

**Ubhay Padangushtasan**

**Marichyasan**

These simple and passive-looking *asanas* have a tremendous element of dynamism. The complete body and various joints, along with different muscle groups, actively participate in these poses. The normally dormant upper back muscles are also toned and stiffness in the lower back, hips, knees and ankles is removed in the process. Forward bends pacify the mind and bring down the heart rate. They can be safely practised by women during menstruation. Warming up from some of the *asanas*, as mentioned in the section on Preparatory poses, is essential. The hamstrings and lower spine should be prepared.

To make it still easier to be able to bend forward, follow the cycle of Halasan-Paschimottanasan of Dynamic Yoga before starting. Breathing is to be kept normal at all times and you can stay in each side of the posture for about a minute. Each cycle can be repeated once again. Twistings and abs/balancings poses can be done more easily after forward bends. Even standing poses may be worth trying. This will help avoid monotony.

# JANU SIRSHASAN

Sides stretched forward

Elbows up

Knee back

Back of leg, heel stretched

## Commencing Poses

## Variations

Bending and turning

Hands stretch and look up

# PARIVRITTA JANU SIRSHASAN

Turn this side

Back of leg, heel stretched

Knee back

## Commencing Pose

## Variation

# TRIANG MUKHAEKAPADA PASCHIMOTTANASAN

One leg in Veerasan

Stretch

## Variations

# ARDHA BADDHA PADMA PASCHIMOTTANASAN

Stretch

One leg in Padmasan

## Variations

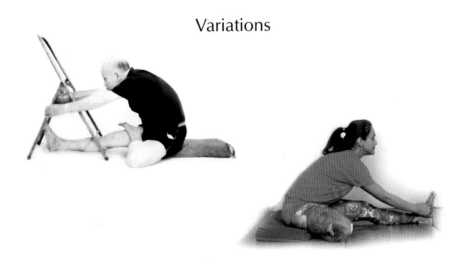

# UPAVISHTA KONASAN

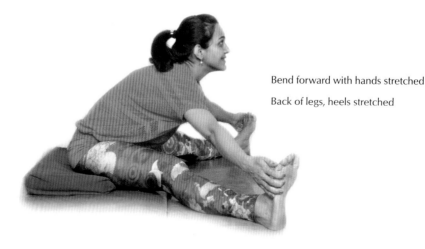

Bend forward with hands stretched

Back of legs, heels stretched

# PARSHVA UPAVISHTA KONASAN

## Commencing Pose

This side turned down

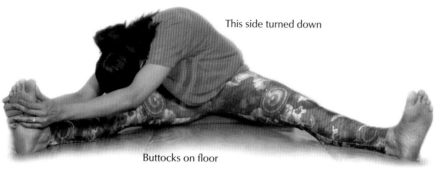

Buttocks on floor

Back of legs, heels stretched

# KROUNCHASAN

Back of leg/heel stretched

Elbows up

Chin on knee

Press down

## Commencing Pose

## Variations

Sitting on height helps

# PASCHIMOTTANASAN

Both sides of armpits stretched

Elbows up

Both legs straight

Back of legs, heels stretched

## Variation

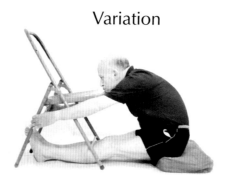

# UBHAY PADANGUSHTASAN

Hands straight

Chin up

Back of legs fully stretched

Spine raised up

## Variation

Using strap

# MARICHYASAN

Chin on knee

# BACK BENDS

**Urdhvamukha Svanasan**

**Pincha Mayurasan**

**Ushtrasan**

**Kapotasan**

**Dhanurasan**

**Urdhva Dhanurasan**

**Viparita Dandasan**

We tend to marvel at the aesthetics and flexibility of back bends while watching a display of *asanas* or seeing photographs. An inquiring mind may, however, ask if this is necessary for yoga and spirituality. If we, like reverse engineering, go backwards to find the final frontier, the answer is yes. If we want to achieve a state of full concentration (*ekagrata*), we should be able to sit quietly and comfortably for a few hours without being disturbed either by the mind or the senses.

The advantages of doing back bends are many. They open the chest to provide more 'space' to the heart and increase the lung volume (by bringing better mobility to the central spine) so that the breath can reach all the way to the pelvic region. The abdomen, diaphragm, organs of the abdominal region and the intestines are well 'toned'. They strengthen the muscles of the spine and its peripheral regions. The neck/shoulder muscles also improve their mobility and residual tensions are relieved. Back bends have contributed tremendously to 'opening' up the 'blockages' in the chakras. You will experience an exhilarating feeling after practising these poses. Make judicious use of the props as shown in the photographs. Follow the sequence of preparatory and recovery poses, as recommended in the suggested weekly plan. Stay in the poses for about 30 breaths and repeat.

# URDHVAMUKHA SVANASAN

Shoulders back

Upper arms turned outwards

Legs stretched

Metatarsals pressed

## Variations

On edge of bed with support

# PINCHA MAYURASAN

## Variation

Shoulders moved
away from wall

Hands and elbows
pressed on floor

Brick between hands
and strap on elbow

## For Beginners

# USHTRASAN

Arms turned out

Hands pressed on heels

Press to floor

## Variations

Elbow on bedhead, resting on bolster

# KAPOTASAN

Chin pressed, metatarsals on mat

## Commencing Poses

## Variation

With chair

# DHANURASAN

Knees kept close to each other

## Variation

Going to the side

# URDHVA DHANURASAN

## Commencing Poses

## Variations

Taking hands to the wall

# VIPARITA DANDASAN

## Commencing Poses

## Commencing Poses

## Variations

On chair

On bed

On chair

Shoulders raised up

Elbows pressed on mat

Back of legs, heels stretched

# ABS & BALANCINGS

**Bhujapidasan**

**Tolasan**

**Bakasan**

**Ashtavakrasan**

**Jathara Parivartanasan**

**Urdhva Prasarita Padasan**

**Navasan**

There is a huge demand these days to develop abdominal muscles (popularly known as six pack abs) and reduce the 'belly'. The belief is that only gymnasiums can cater to this by working on especially designed machines. *Yogasanas* contribute to the overall fitness and health, besides toning up the organs, which are mainly in the abdominal region, they also improve digestion. Yoga, however, does not believe in the 'six pack abs' aspect since it stiffens the diaphragm, which is responsible for our breathing. All types of *asanas*, which makes you bend backwards to stretch the pelvic region, help to keep the diaphragm 'soft'. *Yogis* were said to have used their bodies for 'weight training', here are some examples.

Before attempting these poses, a 'warming up' of the hamstrings (Utthita-Supta Padangustasan) and the lower spine (Uttanasan, Adhomukhaswanasan or Forward Bends) is highly recommended. Stay in the pose for about 20 breaths and repeat.

# BHUJAPIDASAN

Legs taken on shoulders

Elbows straight

## Commencing Poses

Leg on upper arm

Both legs on upper arms

# TOLASAN

## Commencing Pose

# BAKASAN

Buttocks raised

Heels brought closer to buttocks

Knees in armpits

Move forward to balance

Elbows straightened

## Commencing Pose

## Variation

Feet on brick, bolster for head in
case you lose balance

# ASHTAVAKRASAN

Head and body weight shifted forward to balance

Both legs straightened

## Commencing Poses

Take legs to the side

# JATHARA PARIVARTANASAN

Stretch back of legs, heels

# URDHVA PRASARITA PADASAN

Palms pressed on floor

Waist kept on floor and turned sideways

# NAVASAN

# INVERTED POSES

**Sirshasan**

**Sarvangasan**

**Halasan**

**Setubandha Sarvangasan**

**Viparita Karani**

The biggest strength of *yogasana* lies in its inverted poses whose anti-gravity effect have a tremendous positive result, both for the mind and the body. These poses have numerous benefits at the physiological, mental and psychic levels. They help the muscular, skeletal, circulatory, respiratory, endocrine, nervous and digestive systems. In addition, the *prana* is well and equally distributed all over the body. But, above all, even the chakras are activated in tune with the requirements of yoga.

Start gradually and increase the timing, according to capacity, with a maximum of 10 minutes.

# SIRSHASAN

Feet pressed
against each other

Thighs turned inwards

Back of legs stretched

Shoulders raised up

Crown kept on mat

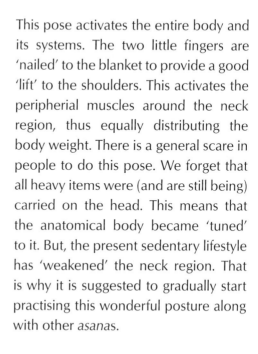

This pose activates the entire body and its systems. The two little fingers are 'nailed' to the blanket to provide a good 'lift' to the shoulders. This activates the peripherial muscles around the neck region, thus equally distributing the body weight. There is a general scare in people to do this pose. We forget that all heavy items were (and are still being) carried on the head. This means that the anatomical body became 'tuned' to it. But, the present sedentary lifestyle has 'weakened' the neck region. That is why it is suggested to gradually start practising this wonderful posture along with other *asanas*.

*Yogis* have used Sirshasan to survive in extreme climatic conditions as the improved blood circulation keeps the body warm in winters and cool in summers. You are advised to not exceed 10 minutes at a time. The pressure on the crown of the head helps to tone up our intelligence. To break the monotony, it may be good to try out the many variations shown here. After doing Sirshasan, it is advisable to do a handstand or Adhomukha Swanasan to relieve the residual tensions in the neck region. People with neck or eye problems and those with high blood pressure should not attempt this pose.

# Commencing Poses

Measuring distance
between elbows

Variation with strap

# Variations

# For Beginners

# SARVANGASAN

*Yogasana*s can never be complete without Sarvangasan; the name itself suggests '*asana* for all parts of the body'. Sirshasan is associated with the sun; Sarvangasan with the moon, as it has a 'cooling' effect on the mind. The advantages of this pose are indeed many. You are invited to test them out and experience them yourself. However, precaution is advised as far as over-stretching or over-straining of the neck muscles is concerned. To avoid this, the shoulders and elbows should be at a height, as shown in the photographs. It also helps you to stay longer in the pose. The variations on a chair or with feet against the wall should also be tried out.

## Commencing Poses

Palms on middle back

Upper arm turned outwards

Eyes pointed to chest

# Commencing Poses

# Variations

# Variations

In Padmasan

Feet on the wall

Leg to the side

Leg to the front

# HALASAN

## Variations

Strap on elbows

# SETUBANDHA SARVANGASAN

The wonderful effect of this versatile pose is the curvature that the spine is brought to. It is excellent to improve posture as it also stretches and brings mobility to the stiff central part (thoracic dorsal) of the spine. It cures numerous posture-related ailments. The abdomen, diaphragm and pelvis are well stretched, allowing the maximum volume of air intake, which is about two-and-a-half times more than the natural air intake. This results in fully charging the body with oxygen (*prana*). The added effect of chin lock (*jalandhar bandha*) facilitates a 'swirl' to give velocity to the inhaled air to go deep into the pelvic region and activate the internal organs. Hence, it is also known as Sarvangasan.

Back of legs, heels stretched

Hands placed on back ribs

Chin close to chest

Arms turned outwards

## Variations

With bolsters under the shoulder

With bolsters

In Padmasan

With bed and bolsters

# VIPARITA KARANI

This pose is best done with legs placed along the wall. By keeping bolsters or pillows under the buttocks, the chest and diaphragm volume is increased as it brings down the breath rate. Like other inverted poses, it also improves blood circulation and reduces the load on the heart. It has the magical effect of calming the mind as soon as you get into the pose. That is why it comes under the category of *mudras*, which work at a more subtle level than *asanas*. The legs also get well rested and varicose veins problems can be arrested and prevented.

## Commencing Poses

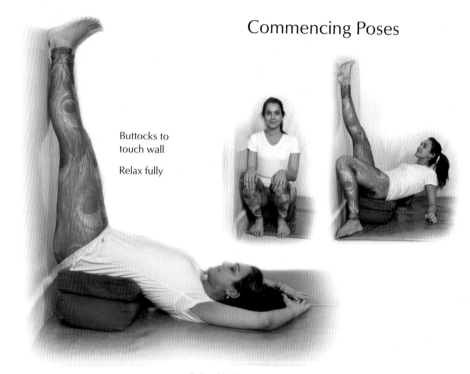

Buttocks to touch wall

Relax fully

## Variations

Shanmukhi *mudra*

# DYNAMIC YOGA

The purpose of *yogasana* practice is to make the body and the mind fit, keeping you free from diseases. This would help to not only fulfil the requirements of daily life but to go beyond to explore the subtle regions within, thus reaching the final frontier of *moksha*. The *asana* practices are mainly static to prepare you to be able to sit in meditation for a long time. But, as mentioned in earlier chapters, getting rid of the toxins in the body is absolutely necessary to become an able *sadhaka* (seeker) or *adhikari* (qualify to be a seeker). With this in mind, yoga guru Pattabhi Jois of Mysore developed Ashtanga Yoga, which became very popular in the West and is now also known as 'Power Yoga'. Here, a series of *asanas* are performed 'dynamically', with the intention that the body becomes more flexible as the muscles become 'warm' and, at the same time, the sweat removes the toxins. Incidentally, his guru, T Krishnamacharya, was also the guru of BKS Iyengar.

The dynamic process of performing some of the *asanas* with a flow (*vinyasa*) is shown in this section. These belong to the Iyengar style of yoga. It was a treat to watch BKS Iyengar practising some of these for 108 repetitions at a stretch! The repetitions can be gradually increased with practise. The Surya Namaskar series is also a part of this 'flow'. But, proper 'warming up' with poses from the Preparatory section and 'cooling down' with those from the Recovery section are highly recommended.

# TADASAN – URDHVADHANURASAN – TADASAN CYCLE

Bending backwards to go down to the floor

# PASCHIMOTTANASAN – HALASAN CYCLE

# SIRSHASAN – BAKASAN CYCLE

# HALASAN – SARVANGASAN – SETUBANDHA CYCLE

# SIRSHASAN –
# URDHVADHANURASAN
# CYCLE

# ADHOMUKHA VRKASHASAN –
# URDHVADHANURASAN
# CYCLE

Beginners can practise with
their back against a wall

Using a wall

# USTRASAN - KAPOTASAN - USTRASAN CYCLE

Using a wall

# HALASAN - SARVANGASAN - SETUBANDHA CYCLE

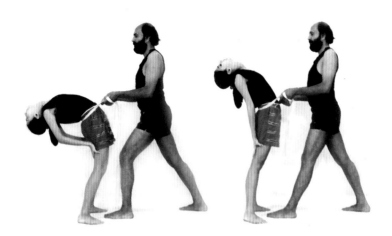

# PRANAYAMA
# POSTURES

Shavasan

Sukhasan

Padmasan

Veerasan

# INDEX